The Highland Clearances

To Ngaire again

The Highland Clearances

People, Landlords and Rural Turmoil

Eric Richards

BIRLINN

This edition first published in 2008 by
Birlinn Ltd
West Newington House
10 Newington Road
Edinburgh
EH9 1QS
www.birlinn.co.uk
Reprinted 2010

ISBN13: 978 184158 542 0

British Library Cataloguing-in-Publication Data
A catalogue record of this book is available from
the British Library

Typeset by Textype, Cambridge
Printed and bound by CPI Cox and Wyman, Reading

Contents

Preface to the 2008 Edition

In September 2006, in balmy weather, I revisited many deserted township sites in the Northern Highlands and tramped around old settlements which have now become well-signposted heritage and tourist attractions. Some have become places of pilgrimage. But the most remote and least preserved sites hold the greatest power and melancholy. Squelching through bogs and clambering over tussocked moorland, it is impossible not to be affected by the knowledge that substantial communities once subsisted for generations in these places. The landscape bears unmistakeable marks of these lives: the physical remains demonstrate the capacity of a departed peasantry to sustain their culture in some of the most difficult terrain in Western Europe. The grandeur of the scenery and the age-old struggle with the elements are irresistibly moving and inspiring. This long-lost achievement of the pre-industrial world is heightened by the fact that, despite all its advances in technology and communications, modern society is now mostly unable or unwilling to dwell in these parts. There are indeed hundreds of deserted houses and townships across the great region of the Highlands and Islands, and this book was written seven years ago to evoke and explain that long and highly controversial historical experience. This task continues and also changes.[1]

Ruins of past rural lives are hardly exclusive to the Scottish Highlands. Similar scenes can be found in my own 'homeland' in North Wales.[2] And within a few weeks of my northern re-familiarisation, I was back in the Antipodes, looking at a no less melancholy landscape of deserted tumbledown farm houses in the parched Australian Outback. Here, the colonists of the 1880s, many of them from Scotland, had reached too far and were eventually forced into retreat from some of the furthest frontiers of the British Diaspora, victims of high mortgage-payments, poor prices and rainless seasons.[3] And then on the high plateau of Central

Otago I saw the sad remnants of the huts and gardens of Chinese colonists created in the 1870s and also abandoned, made redundant by the decline of goldmining in that part of New Zealand.[4] These sites, too, are now well-signposted for the modern tourist.

Such derelict places represented the end of a dream, often accompanied by final desperate efforts to cling on to old attachments. The special potency of the sites in the Scottish Highlands has two particular sources. The 'world we have lost' is more directly conjured up in the Highlands than anywhere else in Britain. Here, dramatically scored in the face of the land, is evidence of a classic pre-industrial form of life. The shape and texture of traditional patterns of life are clearly written in the configuration of the township buildings, in the bare outlines of broken houses and dykes. Similarly the well-defined limits of cultivation exhibit the marks of individual and communal co-operation and a rotation of usage; there are also signs of pre-industrial society among the relics of corn-drying kilns, watermills and the residues of small-scale metal-working and smelting; and the outfield arrangement of communal grazing shows the central role of animal husbandry. Despite the remote and often bleak terrain in which many of these communities lived, it is possible to re-construct the quasi-collective peasant economy persisting stubbornly against the elements and against the external world. The second reason for the particular poignancy of the Highland scene rests in the knowledge that these communities were finally erased, and their people dispersed, in scenes which were often sudden and aggravated.

Consequently I argue that the Highland Clearances were part of the universal story of rural displacement but also contain a particular character, mythology and emotional impact. Yet Highland history remains poorly documented despite the controversy which it always arouses. Nevertheless there are plenty of first-hand descriptions of the more dramatic episodes in the Clearances in this account. These usually took the form of set-piece mass evictions among resistant small tenants, implemented by police or military parties which inevitably led to acts of coercive ejectment, man-handling and injuries. Many cases are described in this book, documented from different angles and sources. They were not unique to the Highlands and were not the main mode of depopulation in the region, merely the most dramatic. The availability of eye-witness accounts has not increased appreciably in the six years which have elapsed since the present account was first published. The story still tends to be dominated by reports by journalists of the 1840s and 1850s, late in the long narrative which stretches back to the 1760s. Lawsuits provide some further evidence of sporadic confrontation between the tenantry and the landlords.

Naturally these dramatic events were much more widely noticed and documented than the slow erosion and gradual displacement of the population over many decades. The relatively quiet dispersal was probably the most common form of population change in the Highlands. And the entire process was always complicated by the concurrent population growth and internal mobility of the region. People leave the land for many reasons, sometimes driven off by unforgiving landlords and creditors, sometimes to escape rural squalor and poverty, sometimes magnetised towards better prospects beyond, at home and abroad. In Britain at large, the retreat from the land has been continuous for 200 years, so that rather less than 5 per cent of the population is now engaged in agriculture. The movement out of agriculture has accelerated at times of depressed primary prices, such as the 1890s and the 1920s. It has been part of the long drift from the land which has been a central and disturbing characteristic of modern times and continues in virtually every society. Humanity at large was once primarily rural; it has now travelled far along the road to universal urbanism. The Highlanders, as this book argues, left their lands for every imaginable reason, but here the extrusive forces, in several forms, were much more urgent and longer lived than in most other places.

The question of how this story should be told is at the very centre of the controversies which have prevailed since the start of the nineteenth century and which have erupted again with typical vituperation in the past seven years. A crucial problem for historians of the Highlands is the persistent imbalance in the documentary sources which have always favoured the literate and the wealthy. As a consequence, the ruins on the landscape carry greater impact on the observer than is usual in historical inter-pretation. Scenes of desertion and demolition and the ravages of time and scavengers summon up traditional ways of life much more effectively than any document or even popular song of the time. In the history of the Clearances it is almost irresistibly tempting to imagine tragic episodes among the stone relics of the old townships. Nor is there any doubt that such episodes disfigured the Highland story, as the early chapters in this book attest. But the sad rickles of the old life do not tell an unambiguous story. Archaeologists have found no evidence of the use of fire by the evicting parties among the deserted townships (even though the relevant documents are often perfectly clear that fire was applied to townships to prevent re-occupation after eviction). Nevertheless the recent work of archaeologists in the Highlands has unearthed the complicated and overlapping layers of occupation and production in the sequences of habitation in the region. The exact chronology of departures and evacuation is rarely clear and the sheer mobility of the old Highland population renders the story inexact at best. Remnants of deserted habitations often relate to post-clearance settlements, and some of the settlements now excavated were created late in the piece, specifically to accommodate people cleared out of older townships. Thus the evidence of the stones is often obscure and can easily mislead and confuse the unwary observer. Some of the ruins I encountered in 2006 had been occupied as recently as 1950.

The idea that animated the first edition of this book remains unchanged; indeed it is reinforced by the current state of play in the unceasing debate about the Highland Clearances. It was designed to provide a modern, sceptical and balanced survey of existing knowledge of the Highland experience. This required a critical sampling of the direct evidence of events and also a sketch of the broad context of what I regard as the essential tragedy of the region as a whole. As well, it scans the controversies and the ideas that have always accompanied the subject. My account repeatedly emphasises the limits of our knowledge in the hope of staving off dogmatism. This recommendation is, to a degree, whistling in the dark because every time the debate erupts it sends the protagonists into extreme versions of the story. At the extremities there is talk of 'genocide' in the Clearances and the no less absurd claim that the Clearances were simply a myth propagated by John Prebble and Ian Grimble. These polemics betray the essentially political agenda which has repeatedly embrangled the history of the Clearances. Ultimately, the story has always been about who should possess and control the uses of the land. Even today, the debate is a variant and recrudescence of what the nineteenth century called 'The Land Question', and it remains a priority in the business of the renewed Scottish Parliament.

The flames repeatedly oxygenated by these public debates have continued to burn, despite the much diminished significance of the Highlands as a proportion of the Scottish and British populations. The persistence of controversy is partly contingent on the very regional status of the Highlands. The experience of the Scottish Highlands is a classic example of regional decline and population dispersal: from as early as 1841 (towards the end of the main period of the Clearances) the population of the Highlands fell absolutely, a decline which continued unabated for another sixteen decades. Meanwhile the Highland economy suffered some of the lowest living standards in the British Isles. This gave the Highlands a distinct and unwanted reputation as an early and striking instance of the fate of certain peripheral regions which gained very little while the rest of the national economy surged forward during cumulative industrialisation. The Highlands became a region of economic and cultural retrogression. Moreover almost every effort to induce economic growth and diversification (of which there were innumerable examples from the 1750s through to the end of the twentieth century), reaped very small benefit to the region. This record of failure reinforced the pessimistic historical argument that it was inevitable that the region simply could not sustain the population levels with which it became saddled by the middle decades of the nineteenth century. The Clearances, in this light, seemed to be the logical, even if a severely rigorous, mechanism for what was, in any case, unavoidable – namely the dispersal of the native population to places where they could achieve employment and living standards regarded as indispensable in the modern world.

Historical perspectives change. After more than a century of demographic retreat, some of the 'regions of retrogression' have, in the past decade, witnessed a surprising resurgence. In parts of 'old rural Europe', Ireland most obviously, the negative trend has at last been reversed: modern economic growth has set in; there has been a substantial growth in *per capita* incomes; population has begun to grow for the first time since 1850 and there is even evidence of net immigration (perplexing for places which have only known emigration). Some of these tendencies have been manifested in the Highlands, most notably around its largest urban centre, Inverness.[5] The new century therefore appears to herald a turning point in Highland prospects which is both exciting and also disconcerting since its explanation remains decidedly uncertain and obscure. The recent reversal in the Highlands also forces into focus new questions about the past. If population and economic indices have been overturned in the present day, we may well need to reconsider the argument that the negative experience of the previous 150 years was actually inevitable and irresistible. This has been a dominant argument in so much of the literature on the Highlands. If the old argument about inevitability is retained, then we need to identify the new and vital variables which have achieved in the past decade what seemed impossible in the previous century. Either way, the recent turnabout in the fortunes of the Highlands is bound to affect the perspective on that historical experience and should soon begin to re-cast the continuing debate about the necessity of the Clearances.

The Highlands today seem to be gripped by a newly positive mentality.[6] One important corollary of the current renaissance (if that is not too strong a word) is that regions such as the Highlands are not necessarily consigned to perpetual marginality and decline. Moreover if the Highlands can revive in the new century, it suggests that this was also a hypothetical possibility in the past. And this, of course, leads to the question of what produced the present happier prospects, as well as what held it back in the past. It becomes, therefore, both a current and an historical question for which there have been few convincing answers, so far.

The present book repeatedly argues that the context of possibilities in the Highlands (both past and present) has always been set much wider than the region itself. The welfare of the Highlands has never been simply a matter of the energy and enterprise of its people and its leaders (as the careers of its emigrants amply demonstrate over the past 200 years). In the nineteenth century the Highlands was constrained most fundamentally by the complicated impact of industrialisation in the rest of British Isles. The Highland experience was generally common to most other rural zones in the British Isles. Similarly, in the early 2000s, the Highlands seems to be following a broader path in common with similar regions in other parts of the old rural zones of Europe. While no one would want to diminish the exceptional character of Highland conditions and the local response to opportunities, these opportunities are often the product of much broader circumstances generated outside the region. In other words the context of change is crucial in historical explanation, and is just as likely to be so in the diagnosis of current changes.

The historical perspective on the Highland Clearances is also realigned by other influences at work in Scotland and elsewhere. One is the burgeoning interest in environmental history which investigates the very long-term trends and consequences in the use and misuse of the land.[7] Our increased knowledge of the forests and animal husbandry in the Highlands, over the past two millennia is helping to re-evaluate the impact of commercial sheep farming in the region. The modern environmental debate also echoes some of the vociferous complaints made by late nineteenth century sheep farmers who experienced declining soil fertility as well as restrictions on muir burning occasioned by the incursions of sporting tenants who added a new layer of competition for the land. Even more influential in the historical debate is the ever-recurring struggle for the control and extension of crofting land in the Highlands: the political campaigns of the past twenty years continue to be couched in terms of the old historical controversies, sharpening the rival indictments of landlords and crofters alike. For more that a hundred years, and certainly since the time of the Napier Commission into Crofting in the 1880s, the past has been invoked to fuel the political contest for the land in the Highlands.[8] One of the themes of the present volume is that particular renditions of the history of the Clearances have exerted a powerful influence on the shape of the modern legislation governing tenure and much else in the region.

Naturally enough, visitors to the Highlands, many from overseas, often seek a clear view of their own family origins in the Highland past, preferably in colourful, if not actually heroic, hues. The idea that history itself changes can be seriously frustrating to anyone wanting the basic facts and a straightforward version of the Highland experience. The mundane realities of the struggle for existence in the past are often disappointing, as though History itself has failed the seeker after roots. The plain historical truth is that most rural origins are relatively commonplace and most moments of departure were incremental and undramatic, even in the Highlands.

Equally disconcerting is the increasing tendency among historians to concentrate their attention on the way history is itself constructed and manipulated for the purposes of each passing interest and generation. In this way recent historians have expended much energy analysing the nature of the public memory of the Clearances and other related issues, notably in the way the subject has been fictionalised, romanticised for genealogical and political purposes, even for northern tourism, and more generally memorialised. This is history at one remove, focusing on the fabrication of the past more than on the contemporary documentation of the events themselves, leaving the impression that there can be no sure foundation for past events. It is nevertheless an instructive and sometimes disconcerting approach to the past and the manner in which it is recruited and moulded by posterity for highly tendentious purposes.[9]

Meanwhile there have been actual advances which will materially benefit the study of the Highland Clearances. The chronology and the geography of the depopulation of the Highlands have never been mapped in detail. The work of rescuing the local stories is now proceeding in a cumulative manner. It remains difficult partly because the definition of 'clearance' is debateable and partly also because many Clearances were never publicised or registered; some were too small and remote for notice. Nevertheless sites are being rediscovered and the landscape reinterpreted, especially in the work of archaeologists and anthropologists in the Highlands. This is a progressive task which will be reinforced further when a new generation of researchers delves more fully in the voluminous records of Highland estates which often contain the inner history of land and tenancy arrangements in the Highlands.[10] Recent historians have also become more alert to the popular and folk memory of the region, carried in song and poetry, now increasingly accessible through the translations of modern scholars. Closer scrutiny has been applied equally to the role of church ministers at the time of the Clearances, men who performed crucial functions in many aspects of Highland life, including the creation of an identifiable 'Crofter ideology' which affected, for example, local responses to new opportunities for emigration.[11] These are bright spots in the evolving historiography of the Highlands, but there is less hope for the people at the bottom of the Highland pyramid, the people without tenure of the land whether before or after the clearances: they included the squatters, the sub-tenants and the *scallags* who were the least visible, yet the most vulnerable and numerous, classes affected by the evictions. History does not offer much chance of their rescue for posterity.

Any history of the Highland Clearances faces widely differing audiences, each with its own expectations. At minimum, it can provide a basic record and chronology of known events and their immediate consequences. This can be made into a narrative, coloured with drama and personality, which may feed a sense of indignation at past wrongs and also apportion blame and responsibility. None of this is difficult but it is reasonable also to expect a realistic and indeed sceptical view of the strengths and weaknesses of the available documentation and the limits of our knowledge. More difficult and less digestible is the effort to balance and convey the problems which encumbered the region during the age of the Clearances – the objective constraints on all sections of Highland society and their different reactions to the problems of the time. This approach can sometimes seem desiccated – a diversion from the stark failures and injustices that characterised the times; it may neglect the many well-meaning efforts to mitigate the problems of the region. Moreover, no account can be complete without proper recognition of the sheer survival of the crofting community, a residual British peasantry, against very harsh odds, a considerable achievement in the late nineteenth century. Similarly, the story needs to give credit to the power of ideology and doctrine in the transformation of Highland society at the time of the Clearances. The strength of ideas is now more fully recognised in the work of historians of the social psychology and popular religion of the Highlands; it is also prominent in the exposure of the notions derived from classical political economy which gripped the minds of the owners and occupiers of the great estates.

The functions of History are increasingly variable. The modern Highlands make good commercial use of the past, but the region also needs a working version of its history. The manner in which the brighter future of the Highlands is to be managed is best served by an earthy understanding of the actual problems the Highlands faced over the recent past. The twin enemies of historical balance are the romantics and the polemicists, and the Highlands have suffered at their hands too long.

Eric Richards
December 2007

Notes

1 Some of these remarks draw on a paper, 'The Highland Clearances Revisited', presented at a seminar in the School of History and Classics, University of Edinburgh, September 2005, and are amplified in Eric Richards, *Debating the Highland Clearances* (Edinburgh University Press, 2007). In the Highlands I was given expert guidance by Dr Malcolm Bangor-Jones and by Jacqueline Aitken and Nick Lindsay of the North of Scotland Archaeological Society, to whom I am a most grateful.

2 See Eric Richards, 'The Australian Option', in Pat Hudson (ed.) *Living Economic and Social History* (Glasgow, Economic History Society, 2001), pp. 302–7.

3 See Donald Meinig, *On the Margins of the Good Earth* (London, 1963).

4 See Michael King, *Penguin History of New Zealand* (Auckland, 2003), pp 210, 369; my thanks are due to Professor Erik Olssen and Dr Annabel Cooper for introducing me to Arrowtown in Otago.

5 Some of the revival is registered in *The Economist*, 27 Nov 2004; 5 Oct 2002, 17 Feb 2001; 5 Jan 2002; 1 May 1999; and more precisely in the recent Censuses.

6 The most optimistic and eloquent overview of current conditions is presented in James Hunter, 'The Highlands: Scotland's Great Success Story', Henry Duncan Prize Lecture, Royal Society of Edinburgh, September 2007. I am grateful to Professor Hunter for a copy of his paper.

7 See for instance, T.C. Smout, *A History of the Native Woodlands of Scotland, 1500–1920* (Edinburgh, 2005).

8 See Andrew G. Newby, *Ireland, Radicalism and the Scottish Highlands, c. 1870–1912* (Edinburgh University Press, 2007).

9 See for instance Paul Basu, 'Pilgrims in a Far Country: North American "roots tourists" in the Scottish Highlands and Islands', in Celeste Ray (ed.), *Transatlantic Scots* (University of Alabama Press, Tuscaloosa, 2005), pp. 286–317.

10 A good recent example is the unpublished PhD thesis of Anne Marie Tindley, 'The Sutherland Estate, c.1860–1914: Aristocratic Decline, Estate Management and Land Reform', University of Edinburgh, 2006.

11 See for example Allan W. MacColl, *Land, Faith and the Crofting Community* (Edinburgh UP, Edinburgh, 2006).

Preface

WHAT WERE THE HIGHLAND Clearances? What actually happened? Were the Highlanders totally evicted? What were the consequences? How much violence was there? Did the Highlanders resist? Were they forced to emigrate? Could it have been different? How did the Highlands compare with elsewhere? Did the landlords gain greatly? What was the mentality of the perpetrators? What happened to the population of the Highlands? How did the Highland Clearances come to be regarded as an act of genocide in Scottish history? How much room for manoeuvre did the landlords possess? Who or what was to blame? Were the clearances really necessary?

These are questions commonly asked about the Highland Clearances. In this account I try to answer them as directly as the historical evidence allows. Because the clearing of the Highlands is one of the most controversial subjects in modern Scotland my answers will not pass unchallenged.

Clearing the Highlands required the ejection of the common Highlanders from the straths and glens and their replacement by cattle, sheep and deer. It was a policy executed over a period of about 100 years by the old and new owners of the great Highland estates. In the process the Highlands were transformed and most of the people reduced to the periphery of the region, and its history then became the byword for landlord oppression and desolation.

Passions about the Highland Clearances still run deep in Scotland and wherever Scottish expatriates think of their home-land. It is also a subject which grips the attention of economists and historians in their efforts to fathom the requirements of economic change in old societies.

This narrative describes the full range of removals that occurred in the region over a century of turmoil. The story easily lends itself to melodrama; this account sticks to contemporary documentation at all points. There can be no denying the essential tragedy of the Highland Clearances and I have no wish to diminish the drama and the distress commonly associated with the events. The main organising notion in this volume is that, in significantly different intensities, the clearances were tragic for almost all parties involved in the great Highland transformation. It was a region overwhelmed with economic and demographic imperatives which caused a melancholia to descend on the community and a yearning for a lost past which still sometimes darkens the northern spirit.

Irish and Scottish history have much in common. An Irish historian has recently complained of the tendency of the general public to 'wallow in the emotional horrors' of, for example, the Great Famine, while academic research makes little impact on the wider world.[1] The same could be said of modern Highland history. The first purpose of *The Highland Clearances* is to establish the story as clearly as the surviving documentation allows. The greatest historical problem is that almost all the written evidence comes from the landowners' side of the story; in compensation it is often necessary to give disproportionate prominence to fragments of evidence from the less well-recorded members of Highland society – the crofters, the cottars, the women, the rioters – often through their petitions, their songs, their ephemera. As well as setting the record as clearly as possible I have tried to explain the circumstances of the Highlands and the framework of conditions which gripped the region like a vice in the age of the clearances.

Acknowledgements

This account draws liberally on my earlier two-volume *History of the Highland Clearances*.[2] I have also called on new work and the help of other historians. There has, for instance, been much new work in the past ten years on the emigration of the Highlanders. Some important work has been undertaken on pre-clearance history,[3] on migratory patterns,[4] on the popular reaction to the clearances captured in the poetic tradition,[5] on deer forests,[6] on the famine administration of the Highlands,[7] and on the contest for the land.[8] There has been new work too on particular districts within the Highlands[9] – and I am especially indebted to the vital work of Dr Malcolm Bangor-Jones.[10] The Australian Research Grants Commission and Flinders University have provided financial assistance. I am also grateful to the late Monica Clough, to Hugh Andrew at Birlinn and to Christopher Helm many years ago, to Dr Hugh Dan MacLennan for the most recent Highland news, to Professor Donald Meek, to Dr Robert Fitzsimons for assistance, and as always to Marian Richards, Ngaire Naffine and the librarians and archivists of the world at large.

Eric Richards
Brighton
South Australia
February 2002

Notes

1 Mary Daly, 'Revisionism and Irish history: the Great Famine', in D. George Boyce and Alan O'Day (eds.), *The Making of Modern Irish History: Revisionism and the Revisionist Controversy* (London: Routledge, 1996), p. 71.

2 Eric Richards, *A History of the Highland Clearances: Vol. I. Agrarian Transformation and the Evictions, 1745–1886* (1982), *A History of the Highland Clearances: Vol. 2. Emigration, Protest, Reasons* (1985); a more focused summary is Eric Richards, 'Fate and culpability in the Highland Clearances', in the *Yearbook of the Scottish History Teachers' Association* (1989), pp. 17–42.

3 See for example Robert Dodgshon, *From Chiefs to Landlords* (Edinburgh, 1998).

4 Charles Withers, *Urban Highlanders* (Edinburgh, 1998); James Hunter, *A Dance Called America* (Edinburgh, 1994); David Craig, *On the Crofters' Trail: In Search of the Clearance Highlanders* (1990).

5 Donald E. Meek, *Tuath is tighearna: Tenants and Landlords* (Edinburgh, 1995).

6 W. Orr, *Deer Forests, Landlords and Crofters* (Edinburgh, 1982).

7 See for example T.M. Devine, *Clanship to Crofter's War* (Manchester, 1994).

8 See especially Ewan Cameron, *Land for the People?* (East Lothian, 1996).

9 See for example Leah Leneman, *Living in Atholl, 1685–1785* (Edinburgh, 1986), Eric Richards and Monica Clough, *Cromartie: Highland Life, 1650–1914* (Aberdeen, 1989); Denis Rixson, *Knoydart: A History* (Edinburgh, 1999).

10 Malcolm Bangor-Jones, *The Assynt Clearances* (Dundee, 1998).

1

The Distant Coronach

I. Suishnish in Skye in 1854

SIR ARCHIBALD GEIKIE WITNESSED a Highland clearance in Skye in 1854. Geikie became a distinguished Scottish geologist who made his reputation with work on the complicated and contentious geology of the west Highlands of Scotland in the late nineteenth century.[1] In later life he wrote his autobiographical *Scottish Reminiscences* in which he looked back over his earliest career among the rocks of his native Skye, an island of great beauty and tragedy as well as scientific fascination. Geikie recalled his youthful geological enthusiasm and knowledge which gained him the attention and friendship of Hugh Miller (himself a pioneer geologist in the Highlands and a challenging political figure in his own right).

Skye in mid-century was pitched into radical economic change which broke into Geikie's own wakening consciousness as a boy. In Kilbride an innocent and vulnerable community was about to be destroyed and Geikie was eyewitness to the infamous clearance at Suishnish in 1854 which, some sixty years after the events, he brilliantly recaptured:

> In those days the political agitator had not appeared on the scene, and though the people had grievances, they had never taken steps to oppose themselves to their landlords or the law. On the whole, they seemed to me a peaceable and contented population, where they had no factors or trustees to raise their rents or to turn them out of their holdings.

It was odd that Geikie made no mention that Skye, like much of the western islands and Highlands, had been repeatedly ravaged by the potato famine during the previous seven years. He continued:

One of the most vivid recollections which I retain of Kilbride is that of the eviction or clearance of the crofts of Suishnish. The corner of Strath between the two sea inlets of Loch Slapin and Loch Eishort had been for ages occupied by a community that cultivated the lower ground where their huts formed a kind of scattered village. The land belonged to the wide domain of Lord Macdonald, whose affairs were in such a state that he had to place himself in the hands of trustees. These men had little local knowledge of the estate, and though they doubtless administered it to the best of their ability, their main object was to make as much money as possible out of the rents, so as on one hand, to satisfy the creditors, and on the other, to hasten the time when the proprietor might be able to resume possession. The interests of the crofters formed a very secondary consideration. With these aims, the trustees determined to clear out the whole population of Suishnish and convert the ground into one large sheep farm, to be placed in the hands of a responsible grazier, if possible, from the south country.

The geologist then recalled the actual moment of eviction:

I had heard some rumours of these intentions, but did not realise that they were in process of being carried into effect, until one afternoon, as I was returning from my ramble, a strange wailing sound reached my ears at intervals on the breeze from the west. On gaining the top of one of the hills on the south side of the valley, I could see a long and motley procession winding along the road that led north from Suishnish. It halted at the point of the road opposite Kilbride, and there the lamentation became long and loud. As I drew nearer, I could see that the minister with his wife and daughters had come out to meet the people and bid them all farewell. It was a miscellaneous gathering of at least three generations of crofters. There were old men and women, too feeble to walk, who were placed in carts; the younger members of the community on foot were carrying their bundles of clothes and household effects, while the children, with looks of alarm, walked alongside. There was a pause in the notes of woe as the last words were exchanged with the family of Kilbride. Everyone was in tears; each wished to clasp the hands that had so often befriended them, and it seemed as if they could not tear themselves away. When they set forth once more, a cry of grief went up to heaven, the long plaintive wail, like a funeral coronach [a Highland dirge], was resumed, and after the last of the emigrants had disappeared behind the hill, the sound seemed to re-echo through the whole wide valley of Strath in one prolonged note of desolation. The people were on their way to be shipped to Canada. I have often wandered since then over the solitary ground of Suishnish. Not a soul is to be seen there now, but the greener patches of field and the crumbling walls mark where an active and happy community once lived.[2]

Geikie's vivid evocation of the Suishnish clearance was an eloquent and graphic testimony to the plight of a small community of peasants on the south-east corner of the island of Skye. It was a singular episode in a remote corner of the region. But it carried most of the main themes in the much wider history of the Highland clearances. Suishnish encapsulated the pathos of the clearances, the tragic end of a simple community in a stark and beautiful landscape overlooking the Atlantic ocean. It highlighted the problem of landlord bankruptcy and irresponsibility. It called attention to the unpreparedness and passivity of the people, to their subsequent emigration, and to the general pathos of the event and its consequences. And Geikie clearly pointed the bone at the landlord's agents, and at the influence of alien forces on this distant place and its fate; his silence on the condition of the people of Suishnish before the clearances invited his readers to assume that, before their dramatic eviction, they had been well-fed, contented and resilient.

In 1854, Suishnish was one of the last episodes in the long history of the Highland clearances; it was also an example of small pre-industrial communities which, across the world, have fallen beneath the implacable demands of economic development. The people of Suishnish stand, in symbolic form, for the rural past which most of the modern world has lost.

II. The rage

The Highland Clearances is one of the sorest, most painful, themes in modern Scottish history. The events have now receded into the distant past, beyond the direct memory of any living person or even their parents. But the passionate indignation lives on, swollen rather than weakened by the passage of time. A rage against past iniquities has been maintained, fed by popular historians and every variety of media construction. A line of denunciation flows from the oral tradition of the early nineteenth century – the *samizdat* of an oppressed and angry people – to the electronic graffiti of the present day in the webs of retrospective indignation. The latter orchestrates the uninhibited passions and prejudices of a worldwide network of Highland sympathisers, many desperate to right past wrongs, some wanting to reverse the steps of their migrant forbears and regain a foothold in their former clanlands. They see the Highlands as a potential escape from the *anomie* of modern society, a beckoning prospect of pre-industrial renewal on ancestral lands. And, somehow, the story of the Highland Clearances also provides fuel to the cause of Scottish nationalism.

During the decades of the Highland Clearances (mainly but not only between 1790 and about 1855) a large proportion of the small tenantry of the region was shifted from their farms. The evictions ('removals' as they were called at the time) affected every part of the Highlands and Islands, from Aberdeenshire in the east to St Kilda on the far edge of the Atlantic shelf, and from Perthshire in the south to the Shetland Isles in the most distant north. The people were shifted off the land to make way for sheep and later for deer; the landlords reaped better rents and reduced the costs of running their great estates. These included some of the greatest territorial empires in the British Isles, and a few of the proprietors were immensely rich. The gap between rich and poor, the powerful and the powerless, was greater than anywhere else in the country. But most of the landowners were men of modest wealth and many were on their uppers both financially and socially.

The people evicted in the classic period of the clearances were often relocated within the estates of the landlord; many shifted off to neighbouring estates or counties; many families eventually made their way to Glasgow, Edinburgh and Dundee, joining the factory workforce or working in the fisheries or harvests on the periphery of their own region; many of the women became domestics for the wealthy new bourgeoisie of urban central Scotland. Others migrated abroad, becoming the Highlanders of eastern Canada,

New Zealand, the United States and Australia. Many nurtured grievances which they passed on to their children and to their children too. The Highlands eventually became a region of depopulation, unable to support either an old population or a modern structure. It became a pastoral satellite of the industrial economy of the south, serving its needs for industrial raw materials, such as wool and kelp as well as mutton and fish. In mid-Victorian times it was partly transmuted into a playground for the rich and, later still, into a sort of national park for the nation at large and its tourists. It signally failed to recover its population or to develop modern industry. This added to the tourist attraction exerted by the twentieth-century Highlands which, naturally, heightened the piquancy of its historical fate.

The question of the Highland Clearances rankles still in the collective memory of Scotland and especially among Scots abroad. This persistent anger is fuelled by a continuing sense of betrayal, and is remarkable for its stamina. Some historians have marvelled at the unhistorical character of the tradition of hatred. The clearances rank with Glencoe and Culloden in the literature of condemnation. It is a subject which regularly raises the chant of 'genocide'.

More than a century after the events themselves the politics of retrospective apology have entered the unending debate. In Ireland a British Prime Minister in 1998 was moved to apologise for British failings in the Great Famine of the 1840s; on the other side of the globe an Australian Prime Minister resisted widespread public pressure to make an apology for European mistreatment of Aborigines in previous generations. In Scotland landowners in April 1998 considered making a collective apology for the Highland Clearances in a transparent effort 'to improve the public image of the landowners'. Auslan Cramb reported that 'the issue of the Clearances keeps coming up. People feel as passionately about them as do former Japanese prisoners-of-war who want the Japanese government to apologise for World War Two. If it is such a stumbling block, we should make an apology. If that is what it takes, we should do it.'[3] One minister referred to current landowners as the 'direct personal beneficiaries of mass eviction'. When the moment of national atonement arrives a nice historical question will arise: who or what was responsible? And if the clearances merit apology would not then every descendant of landlords (Highlander or not, urban as well as rural) need to reconsider the record of centuries of eviction and displacement which mark virtually every system of land and property occupation?

III. Definition

The word 'clearance' was a latecomer to the story. It is defined as 'The clearing of land by the removal of wood, old houses, inhabitants, etc.' and its general usage in this sense is credited to the great observer of London life, Henry Mayhew, in 1851. It was a word with more emotional force than its early synonym, 'eviction', and possessed a different connotation from the landlords' word, 'removal', which was the standard usage in the Highlands until the 1840s. The term was used, on occasion, long before Henry Mayhew spoke of the clearances. In 1804 a sheep farmer in Sutherland faced a clause in his tenancy agreement which, on its expiration, required him to have 'the Farm cleared of any followers (as is now the case)'.[4] In the same county in 1819, in the midst of one of the greatest clearances, an estate agent used the word in the same sense: 'To give you some idea of the extent cleared I subjoin a list of the numbers removed in the different parishes'.[5] One of the church ministers in Sutherland, protesting about these events one year before, had also employed the term: 'From what I know of the circumstances of the majority of those around me,' he wrote, 'since so many were sent down from the heights to clear Sellar's farm, I do not perceive how the great addition, which is intended to be made to their number, can live comfortably as you anticipate'.[6] In 1821 one of the main architects of the clearances, James Loch, spoke of 'the policy of clearing the hills of people, in order to make sheep walks'.[7] In 1827 Duncan Shaw, writing from the island of Benbecula, spoke of the need 'to clear *particular Districts* particularly well calculated for pasture, where the poorest of the people and most of the subtenants reside'.[8] In that year also, the great population theorist Malthus, whose pessimistic influence certainly extended into the Highlands, spoke of the 'clearing of the farms' in Ireland, in his testimony before the Select Committee on Emigration.[9] By 1843, the word 'clearance' had emerged as the general and derogatory term to denote the unsavoury methods of Highland landlords.[10]

But even so, much ambiguity remained in the application of the word. Should the word 'clearance' be reserved for the ejection of entire communities of large numbers of people at a single time, or could it be also applied to individual cases of eviction (or even to the termination of a tenancy agreement)? The Revd Gustavus Aird, in his evidence to the great parliamentary inquiry into Crofting, the Napier Commission in 1883, drew 'a distinction between removal and eviction':

> I call it eviction when they have to go off the estate and go elsewhere. Some of those removed may have been removed out of their places and found places upon the same estate. I make a difference between eviction and removal.[11]

To add to the confusion, William Skene insisted that the proper sense of the term 'clearance' was 'the extension of the land of the large farms and the removal of the former occupants of the land unaccompanied by emigration'.[12] As it happens the phrase 'the Highland Clearances' has become an omnibus term to include any kind of displacement of occupiers (even of sheep) by Highland landlords: it does not discriminate between small and large evictions, voluntary and forced removals, or between outright expulsion of tenants and resettlement plans.

Eviction or clearance in any poor rural society was always a devastation in the life of a landholder. Livelihood, status and prospects all depended on tenure and continuity of occupation: all social relations were determined by the connection with the land. Modern urban society knows little of the tenacity of poor people in their attachment to the land, yet the intense tenurial conflicts are still played out in the present century in the Highlands just as they were, for instance, in the poorer parts of Texas. The clearing of the Highlands was a classic episode in the universal drama of rural transformation. It meant the wrenching of people off lands which they regarded as their own by virtue of ancestral occupation and moral right.

If the historical record is to be called upon, then Scotland itself can provide many lessons in rural displacement both within and beyond its own boundaries. The invasion of northern Ireland by Scottish farmers in the seventeenth century dispossessed hundreds of local people and was among the greatest incursions in the history of the British Isles. Even before, from the fifteenth century onwards, mainland Scots usurped native people in the Shetland Islands. The Scottish crown, having gained the control over the northern islands, encouraged incoming Scots to wrest control over trade and settlement. This created local resentment which was maintained for generations of Shetlanders, yielding an anti-Scottish strain in Shetland history. As early as 1733, Gifford of Busta remarked, in his *Historical Description of the Zetland Islands*:

> At that time many Scottish people came over to it, some as civil, others in an ecclesiastical capacity, and settled here, who in process of time acquired most of the arable land from the antient inhabitants, who became their tenants.[13]

Wherever Scots (including many Highlanders) have emigrated and colonised they have almost invariably displaced indigenous populations, such as the Micmac Indians in Nova Scotia.[14] The ultimate irony in this process was the fact that some of the colonial displacement was accomplished by people who had themselves been usurped, some of them in the Highland Clearances.

Within living memory Scots farmers have invaded English and Welsh agriculture and taken over farms, especially in the south-east but also in Cheshire and Denbighshire. From the 1890s native farmers in Essex experienced extreme difficulty in the depressed conditions of agriculture: 'Indifferent landlords, debt, mortgage and inhospitable markets drove tenant farmers and agricultural labourers off the land'. Old farms, in families for generations, were lost. Into this melancholy rural context, attracted by low rents, came 'hardy immigrants from Scotland and the north, experienced in marginal farming . . . [who] by dint of hard graft and tenacity made them viable'. The Scots became the watchword for efficiency and new methods.

Hence, by 1930, 22 per cent of farmers in Essex were immigrants with a very high proportion of Scots.[15] The locals were simply unable to compete with the incomers (who were probably better educated): it was described as the 'Northern irruption' and the 'Scotch' colonisation of the county. These rural dislocations were on a different scale from the Highland Clearances and no *coronachs* were sounded for the tenant farmers of Essex or Cheshire; no retrospective apologies were demanded of the Scottish nation on behalf of the landless descendants of the native farmers. Yet these rural turnovers were, in effect, latter-day clearances in favour of Scottish farmers who were able to farm the land more efficiently than the natives. The irony was almost certainly lost on the aborigines of Essex, though they too were victims of the flux of rural change, abandoned to the considerable condescension of Scottish posterity.[16]

IV. The rage maintained, 1770–2000

The intensity of the passions generated about the clearances cannot be doubted. The flame burned from the start and then erupted throughout the events and has been kept intermittently fuelled to the present day.[17] Anxiety about the fate of the Highlanders accompanied the transformation of the region from as early as the 1750s. When relatively large numbers of Highlanders and Islanders emigrated in the 1760s and 1770s public opinion immediately blamed the landlords for imposing a new degree of commercialism on the people, raising their rents and snapping the old ties of clan loyalty. Large parties of Highlanders left for the American colonies, often led by the middle cadres of Highland society, the tacksmen who were large leaseholders who normally sublet land to the lower echelons of the tenantry. Facing rising rents which themselves reflected the growing pressure on land resources in the Highlands, the tacksmen took off for America, often cocking a snook at the landlords as they departed. Some landlords took fright and thought they would lose not only their rents but the population on which the entire economy ultimately depended. When, by 1780, commodity prices increasingly favoured cattle and then sheep production the pressure redoubled, just as it did in other parts of Britain.

After his illustrious tour in 1772, Dr Samuel Johnson was one of the first to express national apprehension for the future of the Highlands. He vividly reported the 'general dissatisfaction which is now driving the Highlanders into the other hemisphere.'[18] The people, according to another source in 1770, were being forced to emigrate by 'the Rapacity and oppression of their masters at home'.[19]

Hector St John de Crevecoeur's *Letters*, published in 1782, spoke of the Hebrides and the Orkneys as 'unfit for the habitation of men: they appear to be calculated only for great sheep pastures. Who, then, can blame the inhabitants of these countries for transporting themselves thither?' He added that 'the Hebrides appear to be fit only for the residence of malefactors'. It would be better for the British government to transport convicts to the Hebrides than to Virginia or Maryland:

> The English government should purchase the most northern and barren of those islands [. . .] it should send over to us the honest, primitive Hebrideans, settle them here on good lands as a reward for their virtue and ancient poverty, and replace them with a colony of her wicked sons [. . .] Two essential ends would be answered by this simple operation: the good people, by emigration, would be rendered happier; the bad ones would be placed where they ought to be.[20]

By the 1810s, criticism of Highland landlords rang throughout the land. General David Stewart of Garth painted a picture of a romantic and innocent society being destroyed by the mercenary and disloyal landlord class who were evicting their people ruthlessly and without regard for common decency. The *Military Register*, a London journal, tried to provoke the evicted Highlanders to resist the introduction of the alien sheep farmers who were monopolising so much of the land in the Highlands. In terms of effective opposition to landlord policy, the results were meagre.

One of the men best acquainted with the Highlands in the age of the clearances was the road engineer Joseph Mitchell whose

Reminiscences were published in 1883–4 at a time of great agitation against landlords in the Highlands.[21] (His books were virtually suppressed and he died soon after, thereby avoiding legal action.) His view of the clearances was negative. As he put it:

> Large tracts of land were let to southern sheep farmers, and the aboriginal occupants were ruthlessly cleared away amidst much distress and misery. Many of the Highlanders went south, and betook themselves to industrial occupations, and a large number emigrated to America; but the chief portion were removed to crofts on the sea shore, where they afterwards eked out a wretched existence by the cultivation of potatoes and by fishing.

Mitchell, who was also prepared to blame the indolence of the Highlanders for part of their fate, mainly attacked the land agents, the factors, for the blighting of the Highlands, men invested with too much local authority by a landlord class which had distanced itself from the administration of its estates, and thereby lost its role as guardians of the people.

One man in particular, Patrick Sellar, came to serve as the all-purpose target of condemnation, personifying the entire tragedy. Sellar was the sheep farmer-cum-factor on the Sutherland estate during the time of the most ambitious of all the clearances in the 1810s. He implemented a series of evictions in 1814 which eventually caused the people of Strathnaver to accuse him of a string of atrocities against life and property. He was brought to trial in Inverness in April 1816 on many charges but especially that of the culpable homicide (equivalent to manslaughter) of victims during his evictions. Sellar was exculpated, but the case against him continued in the written and oral annals of the Highlands down to the present day. Few in Scotland believed him innocent, though the verdict was not challenged at the time. Consequently Sellar became the target of the accumulated and ritualised indignation of posterity against the clearances.

The most effective evocation of Sellar was Neil Gunn's famous novel *Butcher's Broom* (1934), which satirised Sellar in the figure of Heller and argued that the community and culture of the Highlanders was destroyed by the clearances. Fionna MacColla's

And the Cock Crew (1945) was a passionate criticism of the Calvinist ideology and attitudes which left the people vulnerable to the policy. Sellar became the personification of factorial evil and avarice in the children's story by Kathleen Fidler, *The Desperate Journey* (1964). Iain Crichton Smith's *Consider the Lilies*[22] was a more substantial and convincing novel, but did not pretend to historical accuracy. It dealt with the clearances through the eyes of an old woman confronting an eviction and depicted Sellar as an outsider, 'a short fat man with piercing eyes and thin lips [sic], working for the Duke [of Sutherland] whom he despises'. Moreover, Sellar seemed to conform to a racial type too, for 'His head wasn't Highland'. Sellar is depicted as quite young, vigorous and powerful, speaking fast in English and riding a white horse, while she is old and frail, slow in comprehension and submissive. The novel notably attacked Scottish Presbyterianism and the role of the ministers, particularly their falsity and hypocrisy during the removals. Crichton Smith also wrote a play about the trial of Sellar, in which he chose to set the events in Hell. He wrote a poem on 'The Clearances' in which he used an 'uncharacteristically harsh voice' to denounce Sellar:

> Though hate is evil we cannot
> but hope your courtier's heels in hell
> are burning.[23]

The savagery of the writing against Sellar was reinforced by the work of Ian Grimble who, like Alexander Mackenzie a century before, built his case on the succession of anti-Sellar polemics from Stewart of Garth onwards. Grimble heightened his case against Sellar by drawing a specific modern parallel. Sellar's crimes against the people of Strathnaver, he said, were to be ranked with those of Heydrich, the man who perpetrated unspeakable acts against the Jews in Prague in the Second World War. Grimble's contribution was, therefore, to make Sellar the centrepiece of the popular account of the clearances, which brought the events into comparison with the Holocaust, and serious talk of the 'genocide' of the Highland people. David Craig, more recently, has compared the evictions to 'the shipping-off of the Polish and other Jews in cattle trucks'.[24]

By the 1990s, the entire Highland story, in one influential view, could be rendered down into 'a war between two Scotlands. It was the mercantile, Protestant, Scots-speaking Lowlanders who wanted to destroy their feudal, cattle-rearing, Catholic Gaelic-speaking neighbours and helped the English to do so.'[25] Sellar's reputation expanded so that, in 1996, it was claimed that he moved 8000 people out of Britain's largest county to make way for sheep, leaving it 'the deathly desert it is today'. John Macleod described Sellar's tactics in *Highlanders*, his published history of the Gaels: 'Violent assault: men, women and children beaten with staves, young women kicked in the genitals. Wanton destruction: the burning of houses and effects. Grand larceny: the seizing of cattle and other livestock. And murder.'[26]

Only a few doubts remained. Between the same covers of the *New Companion to Scottish Culture*[27] the Sellar episode in 1814 was represented by one contributor as 'one of the most emotive and searing moments in the history of Gaelic Scotland', while another pointed out that the accusations of brutality were not proved in court, though they had certainly entered the popular image of the clearances. A further entry in the same volume, on 'Supernatural Beliefs', established that Sellar, in tradition, would have been 'eaten alive by worms' on account of his crimes.[27] Patrick Sellar's grave in Elgin Cathedral became 'the perennial target for mucus, divots and paint – and much worse when to hand'.[28] Before the end of the twentieth century, the global mail system was abuzz with electronic graffiti directed against Patrick Sellar.[29]

By the end of the twentieth century there were no identifiable descendants of Sellar in the north. But a large though diminishing percentage of the old Sutherland estate remained in the hands of the descendants of the Countess of Sutherland who had ordered the clearances in the 1810s. Thus the modern Sutherland family bore the brunt of the public condemnation and experienced public abuse and insult throughout the 1980s and 1990s. They resented the burden of the past which had been thrust upon them. As one interviewer reported in 1996, 'Today the Sutherland Family is fed up with the clearances and with being held responsible for its ancestors'.[30]

The stamina of these hatreds was predictably revived as the new Scottish Parliament was established in 1999. High on the agenda of some Scots was the imminent prospect of reversing 'the feudal landowning system to help communities to buy land from the noble families that have controlled it since the Middle Ages'. It was reckoned that 14 per cent of Scotland was still owned by twenty-one nobles and new legislation could release the land to the people. As one observer put it, 'Since the Clearances, Scotland has been divided into astonishingly large chunks that can be freely bought and sold and left to degenerate into depopulated wilderness'. The clearances were the worst expression of 'private landlordism' and allegedly the root cause of so much modern desperation in the Highlands.[31]

To say that the lairds of the Highlands have experienced a bad press would be a gross historical understatement. It is a record of barely relieved vilification and abuse: the clamour for retribution and restitution is undiminished.

V. Landlords

Popular landlords are as rare as hen's teeth. Their functions and utility to society rarely seem commensurate with their rent extractions, command of resources and local authority. Their place in the social pyramid often seems ornamental and exploitative. This is partly because land is commonly regarded as unlike other types of investment and different from other types of property. Landlords are somehow unlike other rentiers and producers. So when a factory owner or a commercial bank lays off employees it generally seems a less aggravated action compared with the removal of a tenant by a landlord. The social construction of landlordism is different because social responsibilities are assumed to be integral to landowning.

Highland landlords have become figures of hatred, ogres even among landlords. The clearance of the Highlands was one of the great tragic anger-generating episodes in modern British history, to be invoked in the same breath as the Irish Famine, Peterloo, the enclosure movement and factory conditions in the Industrial Revolution. For here were poor people shunted off their lands to make way for sheep in scenes of destruction and aggravated inhumanity. Hence the legacy of impotent rage, an incredulous incomprehension that this was in any sense necessary or fair; the raging anger at the ruling class and detestation of London and Edinburgh for allowing it to happen; and the total disbelief that the Highlands could not accommodate the people. The Highlanders meanwhile have become historically photogenic and the eviction of the clansmen takes on an aura of pathos greater than similar events which were commonplace in the rest of the country.

There were of course landlords before the clearances. It is not certain that they were any more tender to their tenantry than their successors in the age of the clearances. In the long perspective the clearing of the Highlands inevitably revolves about the morality of landlord actions and their responsibility for the economic condition of the Highlands through the century of change.

In the following chapters certain central questions recur and intersect with these judgements about morality and economics. The first concerns the condition of the Highlands before the clearances. If it can be demonstrated that life had been relatively secure and prosperous, then the case against the clearers is magnified.

The second question involves the demographic dimension: that is, the impact of population change in the region which parallelled the clearances and cast a great influence on the welfare of the region. At the time this issue was dominant in the arguments employed to justify the evictions. Latter-day critics of the landlords cannot escape grappling with the population question.

The third question concerns the hypothetical alternatives to the Highland Clearances: what, indeed, would have happened if the policy had not been implemented? Could the old society of the Highlands have coped with the twin challenges of population growth and structural change? No other part of Britain was able to do so. In reality many different solutions were attempted in the Highlands in the age of the clearances and indeed have been ever since.

But the prior question is, what happened in the clearances? In other words, what does the evidence reveal?

Notes

1 See David R. Oldroyd, *The Highland Controversy: Constructing Geological Knowledge through Fieldwork in Nineteenth-Century Britain* (Chicago: Chicago University Press, 1990).

2 Archibald Geikie, *Scottish Reminiscences* (Glasgow, 1906), pp. 224–7.

3 *Daily Telegraph*, 27 April 1998.

4 R.J. Adam (ed.), *Papers on Sutherland Estate Management* (Scottish History Society, 2 vols., Edinburgh, 1972), vol. II, p. 30.

5 Stafford County Record Office (hereafter SCRO), Sutherland Collection (hereafter D593): D593/K/Suther to Loch, 29 May 1819; Loch to Orme, 10 April 1821.

6 Revd Mackenzie to Loch, March 1818, quoted in Alexander Mackay, *Sketches of Sutherland Characters* (Edinburgh, 1889), p. 208.

7 SCRO, D593/K/Loch to Orme, 10 April 1821.

8 Scottish Record Office (hereafter SRO), GD 201/4/97, Duncan Shaw to Alexander Hunter, 25 February 1827.

9 Parliamentary Papers (hereafter PP), 1826–7, V, p. 316.

10 [Hugh Miller], *Sutherland As It Was and Is* (Edinburgh, 1843). See also *The Times*, 15 May 1845.

11 Report of the Commissioners of Inquiry into the Condition of the Crofters and Cottars in the Highlands and Islands of Scotland, PP, XXXII–XXXVI (1884) (hereafter Napier Commission), Evidence, p. 134.

12 William Skene, *Celtic Scotland* (3 vols., Edinburgh, 1880), vol. III, p. 376.

13 Quoted by Brian Smith, 'Lairds and "Improvement" in 17th and 18th century Shetland', in T. M. Devine, (ed.), *Lairds and Improvement in the Scotland of the Enlightenment* (Dundee, 1979).

14 See James Hunter, *A Dance Called America* (Edinburgh, 1994), p. 237 ff.

15 See Alun Howkins, *Reshaping Rural England*, pp. 150–52.

16 Kenneth Neale, *Essex: A History* (Chichester, 1997), p. 141. See also Primrose McConnell, 'Experiences of a Scotsman on the Essex Clays', *Journal of the Royal Agricultural Society of England*, 3rd series vol. 2 (1891), pp. 311–25. See 'Scottish farming in Essex', *Country Life Illustrated*, 29 September 1900, pp. 396–8, and John Hunter, *The Essex Landscape*, (Chelmsford, 1999) pp. 166–8.

17 For an historical survey of opinion on the Highland Clearances, see Richards, *History* II, Part One.

18 Quoted by Alex Murdoch, 'Emigration from the Scottish Highlands to America in the eighteenth century', in *British Journal of Eighteenth-Century Studies*, 21 (1998), pp. 161–2.

19 Quoted by John L. Campbell, *Songs Remembered in Exile* (Aberdeen, 1990), p. 23.

20 Murdoch, op. cit., 162.

21 Joseph Mitchell, *Reminiscences of my Life in the Highlands* (2 vols., originally published privately in 1883 and 1884, reprinted in 1971), p. 20.

22 Iain Crichton Smith, *Consider the Lilies* (Edinburgh, 1968, edn. 1987).

23 Quoted in Lorn Macintyre, 'A Rare Intelligence', in Colin Nicholson (ed.), *Iain Crichton Smith: Critical Essays* (1992), p. 158.

24 David Craig, *On the Crofters' Trail* (1990) quoted in Paul Basu, 'Narratives in a Landscape' unpublished M.Sc. thesis, University College, London 1997, p. 21.

25 Review of Prebble in *The Times* 1996.

26 The *Guardian Weekend*, 12 October 1996, p. 36.

27 David Daiches (ed.), *New Companion to Scottish Culture* (1993), pp. 54, 318. The folklore view is exemplified by Alexander Campbell, *The Romance of the Highlands* (Aberdeen, 1927), p. 263.

28 Letter of Robert Dryden to *Scotsman*, 21 October 1994.

29 See Richards, *Patrick Sellar and the Highland Clearances* (Edinburgh 1999), passim.

30 Auslan Cramb, *Who Owns Scotland Now?* (Edinburgh, 1996), p. 162.

31 *The Times*, 29 December 1998.

2

Classic Highland Clearances: Glencalvie and Strathconan

S OME HIGHLAND CLEARANCES WERE small in scale and were scarcely recorded at all, either at the time or later. Some were achieved by attrition – a continuing erosion of the old communities in the inland glens until entire districts were left deserted. Landlords could simply terminate an annual tenancy; or one family after another could be evicted as their rents fell into arrears; or a married offspring might be required to leave the house of his or her parent according to the new rules of the estate; an entire township could be run down year by year, usually without resistance or even complaint, without demolition or violence or publicity. They were small events but the cumulative effect was eventually decisive: the population was dislodged and diminished; the old world was replaced by the new order of sheep, deer and tourists, some of them royal.

In reality the best-known clearances were not the silent dispersions of this sort. The historical account of the clearances is dominated by those which attracted immediate attention or entered the angry memory of the people dispersed, and captured in satire, song and the oral recollection. They were sudden and involved large numbers of people in a single season of eviction. Glencalvie and Strathconan were two infamous episodes in the mid-nineteenth century, relatively late in the piece, and both on the eastern edge of the Highlands. They were the type of sensational clearance which attracted widespread publicity; the events at Glencalvie and Strathconan can be reconstructed in vivid detail.

I. Glencalvie

'Unconditional compliance' was the most common reaction of the people of the Highlands when served with papers to quit their lands. This was true of the people of Glencalvie whose clearance in 1845 reached public attention only because the local Free Church ministers, men already at war with the established church and with most of the landlords, blazoned their plight in the *Scotsman*. The story came to the notice of *The Times* which despatched north one of its investigatory 'commissioners' to cover the story.

In 1845 clearances were raging throughout the county of Ross and it was reported that 400 families (perhaps 2000 people in all) had received notices to quit in that year. The *Ross-shire Advertiser*, in Dingwall, commented:

> Whether this extensive number of removals is partly or in whole mere shifting of the occupants for the purpose of improved arrangements, or the entire ejection of small tenants, we have not ascertained, but the fact of the notices being served is undoubtedly correct.[1]

This was a crucial distinction. Some estates in the Highlands cushioned the change by the provision of alternative land for the displaced people, though resettlement rarely satisfied the people or the watchful public. Some landlords helped their departing people to migrate south or overseas, and they too were often abused for these poor efforts to salvage their consciences and their reputations. Other landlords simply evicted outright – the tenants were ejected into the world without compunction.

With the removals at Glencalvie impending, the *Scotsman* ran the story under the banner headline 'HEART RENDING CASES OF DISTRESS' and described the plight of the ninety 'crofters' (a term usually applied to small tenantry already resettled on an estate) and tenants who were to be removed on 12 May 1845. They comprised eighteen families who lived in the straths of Amatnatua, Greenyards and Glencalvie, in the parish of Kincardine in Easter Ross. Each of the families possessed a cottage, and they were to be shifted specifically to make room for sheep farmers and sportsmen.

The extraordinary step taken by the Glencalvie people was to appeal directly to the general public through the newspapers. They got up a petition and, with the sponsorship of five Free Church ministers, placed it in the *Scotsman*. It sought public subscription for their future re-settlement. Their case was argued in detail:

> The Petitioners and their forefathers from time immemorial – indeed for centuries – have occupied their small farms and crofts under various proprietors; but though their rents have been paid and no offence charged against them, they are duly warned that by force of law they must be removed on *Monday the 12th day of May* ensuing to make way for strangers.

The petition explained that there were many aged and infirm persons among them who could not possibly emigrate to America, even if they possessed the resources and wished to do so. There was no employment in the north of Scotland, and the menfolk could not leave their dejected dependants until they secured alternative residences. They pointed out that, as soon as the notices to quit had been received, some of the people had trekked over the counties of Inverness and Sutherland in search of small farms or even places for temporary huts, but all in vain. Hence it was planned to create an extraordinary asylum for the refugees in the churchyard of Glencalvie 'underneath whose surface lie the ashes of their ancestors as well as relatives recently buried there'. Meanwhile the ministers would seek charitable supplies and other permanent accommodation.

The advertisement placed by the ministers to accompany the petition spoke unambiguously of 'the grasp of powerful invaders' on the land of the community. One of the five ministers had personally undertaken to give over his manse at Bonar Bridge for the accommodation of the petitioners. This minister, the Revd Gustavus Aird, voiced trenchant criticism of the landlord:

> Matters have really come to an awful pitch, when beings possessed of immortal souls, originally created after the divine image, are driven out of their homes and fatherland to make way for fir and *larch plants, deer, roes, moorgame, partridges* and *hares*. Nothing shall give me greater pleasure than to have my name down as a receiver of any sum of income, or meal, or anything which may be given to the poor people. If

matters come to the extremity, I know there are some of them who, from great age and infirmity, could not *endure one night – under* a *tent*; yet so far as this *house will furnish accommodation* for such, they *shall have* it. His be the blessedness pronounced by heaven on those who consider the poor.

The people of Glencalvie claimed that they had approached the factor (in place of the absentee landlord) to delay the clearance, but he had reaffirmed his intention to proceed at the declared time.

They remarked that they did not ascribe to their landlord any severity other than what necessarily attaches to a system of clearing the Highlands of human beings in order to make way for sheep, now too often acted on. The law of the land allows him to separate the Petitioners from the soil, whatever may be the consequences.

This statement signalled a growing popular awareness by mid-century of the political implications of landlord behaviour and it reflected the vigorous influence of the Free Church ministers. The petitioners conceded that they had been given full notice of removal, but alternative accommodation had been impossible to find and they pleaded for a reprieve. They were prepared to yield to the authority of the law, but appealed to the public at large, seeking money for tents and for their general relief. The charity would be channelled through their nominated Free Church ministers in the north, and in both Edinburgh and Glasgow.[2]

The pathos of the Glencalvie petition made a strong impression on the public mind in the south and the newspapers recognised that it had the makings of an excellent story. Public sympathy for the people quickly prompted considerable subscriptions for their relief, but the great problem was the provision of alternative accommodation. A neighbouring landlord, Munro of Teannich, was able to offer two cottages on his estate for the destitute, but this was evidently not nearly enough.

The owner of the Glencalvie estate was Major Charles Robertson of Kindeace who was in Australia with his regiment. The family was Highland and heavily involved in the Army: Robertson's father held commissions in Highland regiments and served as a major in the attack on Java. The Robertsons included a planter in Jamaica and another in Demerara (both died from yellow fever), another was a medical officer with the East India Company (who died of lockjaw from a snake bite); one was a merchant in London, and another in New Orleans; another was employed by Trinity House in London. Charles Robertson himself married a Chisholm, sister of the infamous clearer of Greenyards.

Like so many Highland families, the Robertsons were pillars of the Empire, and had little time for their own domestic responsibilities. The Kindeace estate was effectively in the hands of the factor, James Falconer Gillanders of Highfield, who had already been employed by several proprietors in the rigorous business of clearing small tenants from their lands, in which work he developed a reputation similar to that of Patrick Sellar. In May 1845 he organised the clearance of sixteen families from Newmore. Since 1841 he had been shifting 'some hundreds of families' out of Strathconan, and was also employed in similar but less extensive work on arable lands in the Black Isle. He had been engaged in the business of the Glencalvie estate for several years and in 1842 had issued the original notices to quit. A man of stubborn resolve, Gillanders was not easily deflected, but the adverse publicity about his work at Glencalvie in April 1844 persuaded him to delay the clearance for two weeks.[3]

The Glencalvie affair attracted a much stronger light when *The Times* fostered the story and directed its reporter to the scene of the removals. He described the circumstances of the case in much more thorough detail than the local accounts. The events (now being described as 'clearances') were, he wrote, reminiscent of the great and infamous Sutherland clearances of the 1810s[4] both in their inhumanity and in their devotion to William Cobbett's derided 'feelosophy' (meaning Political Economy). It was, said this account, a classic example of a landlord, in pursuit of a few pounds, creating inconceivable misery and hopeless destitution among a people who had been industrious and peaceable peasants. The district had already been subject to clearances for several years and the population had already fallen. The people paid an annual rent of £55.10.0 for very poor land which, he contended, would fetch hardly £15 in England. The people of Glencalvie had paid their rent without fail by way of their production of potatoes, barley and a few stock. There was no crime in the district and none of the people were on the Poor Roll. The strath had yielded many fighting men during the war against Napoleon. On all these scores it was a blameless community. The initiative for the clearance had come from the factor, Gillanders, who had a wide reputation as a decisive removalist on other estates before he tackled Glencalvie. Gillanders had judged that the land would be better arranged, and more lucratively, as a single sheep walk.

According to *The Times* reporter, the forebears of the Glencalvie families had occupied the land in question for half a millennium. He recounted the earlier efforts of clearance on the Glencalvie estate, which had followed the common pattern of Highland resistance.[5] In February 1842 Gillanders had advertised the Glencalvie lands as a sheep farm for occupation in the following year. The people had pleaded against their removal and had recruited the support of the new minister, Gustavus Aird. Despite their pleas, an attempt was made in March 1843 to serve the notices of removal upon the Glencalvie people. In this instance the constables were waylaid by the womenfolk and their legal papers were set afire beneath their noses. Recounting this story, *The Times* reporter suggested that this was a relatively mild and perfectly natural response by the people. It was at this time that the people offered to pay a higher rent, and further, offered a higher rent than any sheep farmer, but without success. Factors much preferred to transact with one sheep farmer than with a mass of small tenants: 'It is said that the factor would rather have one tenant than many, as it saves him trouble!', commented *The Times* reporter.

In 1844 Gillanders had tried again to expel the Glencalvie people. He 'tricked' them into the service of the notice and, further, promised to give them £100 when they actually quitted, and pointed out that they would be entitled to take their house timbers with them. The *Glasgow National*, reporting in August 1844, pointed out that the people had paid every farthing of rent, even during the most recent famine in 1836–7. They had been losing their customary rights for over a century and they were now in a state of terror.[6] But *The Times* reporter acknowledged that the proceeding had been conducted with temperance and moderation – that is, if 'the excessive harshness of removing the people at all' were discounted. Gillanders allowed the people to stay until 25 May 1845 and claimed that they had all arranged alternative accommodation.

The Times reporter discovered that only six of the eighteen families had gained refuge – mostly on extortionate and squalid terms in the neighbouring villages of Bonar Bridge and Edderton. The rest were in a condition 'hopeless and helpless', having perambulated every neighbouring estate in vain for refuge. Landlords were reluctant to take in such refugees at this time or to give any cottage to likely paupers, because of the impending passage of the Scottish Poor Law bill (which would require landlords and farmers to support paupers throughout Scotland). The Glencalvie people 'did not know where to go to, and what to do to live'. *The Times* correspondent denounced the entire affair as a wanton abuse of landlord power, made worse by the fact that there did not seem to be any immediate financial advantage in the change. He testified to the 'widespread indignation that such cases aroused in the Highlands' which, he believed, failed to transform itself into turbulent resistance to the law because of the pacifying influence of religion.[7]

The Times treatment of the Glencalvie clearance was part of a journalistic campaign which, on the eve of the Parliamentary debate on the system of poor relief in Scotland, exposed existing conditions among the poor in many parts of the Highlands. *The Times* commissioner wrote a series of exposés of Highland landlordism and Glencalvie was the most extreme example of proprietorial behaviour. These reports were quoted at length in a debate in the House of Commons in mid-June 1845 when Sharman Crawford referred directly to the 'dispossessment of the tenantry' at Glencalvie. He said that this case demonstrated conclusively that the landlords were barbarous exterminators of the people and were totally unfitted for the care of the poor and the organisation of poor relief.[8]

But the Glencalvie episode was not yet completed: the people awaited their final ejection. At the end of May 1845 they left their cottages and set up camp in the churchyard. *The Times* reporter returned to Ardgay and to the churchyard. He emphasised the acquiescent demeanour of the people in their humiliation:

> Were any such clearances attempted in England, I leave you to conceive the excitement which it would be certain to create – the mob processions, the effigy burnings, and the window smashings, with which every instigator and instrument in so heartless a scene would be reminded that there are principles of action which are thought more honourable, more worthy, and which make living amongst our fellows more pleasant, than mere money grubbing.

The Highlanders, he remarked, had been completely mild, passive, broken in spirit and unremonstrative, despite 'this heartless wholesale ejectment'. In this judgement he was not entirely accurate: there was a record of sporadic resistance to clearance (notably in 1792, 1813 and 1820–1) and the people of Glencalvie themselves had shown mild resistance in 1843. Moreover, the contrast with England was poorly conceived: the enclosure movement in the eighteenth century had produced very little violent reaction from the English agricultural classes though, of course, wholesale ejectments in England were not common.[9]

The Times' correspondent visited the strath of Glencalvie on a Sunday to find the people:

> assembled on a hillside to listen to psalms from their elders, the women all neatly dressed in net caps, and wearing their blue bonnets, and having their shepherd's [sic] plaids wrapped around them. This was their only covering, and this was the Free Church. There was a simplicity extremely touching in this group on the bare hill side, listening to the psalms of David in their native tongue, and assembled to worship God – many of them without a home.

At this service there were gathered about 250 people drawn from the adjacent straths. On that day the local established church was able to draw a congregation of ten. It was a fair reflection of the contest of the kirks in the Highlands in the years after the Disruption. *The Times* reporter then described the scene of the Glencalvie refugees: 'Behind the church, in the courtyard, a long kind of booth was erected, the roof formed of tarpaulin stretched over poles, the sides closed in with horse cloths, rugs, blankets, and plaids. On inquiry I found this was the refuge of the Glen Calvie people'. The group now comprised eighty persons: twenty-three less than ten years of age, seven in bad health, ten older than sixty years and eight young married men. They had been accommodated in the churchyard since the previous Saturday. The report continued:

> I am told it was a most wretched spectacle to see these poor people march out of the glen in a body, with two or three carts filled with children, many of them mere infants, and other carts containing their bedding and other requisites. The whole countryside was up on the hills watching them as they steadily took possession of their tent.

This therefore was the moment of clearance. It was a powerful picture of a broken community among the gravestones, cowering under the will of a neglectful landowner and his rigid factor. The newspaper accounts did nothing to diminish the squalor and pathos of the event; they left vivid images of children clustering around the campfire, of the congested sleeping arrangements inside the tents and of the dejected countenances of the mothers. The reports spoke of 'the melancholy picture of the poor children thoughtlessly playing round the fire, pleased with the novelty of all around them'. The agents, who were responsible for paying the people the sums of compensation for their stock, treated them with kindliness. There had been no disturbance and each family received about £18 for their stock and to assist their suggested emigration. It was relatively generous assistance by the landlord and a substantial sum of cash for any ordinary family in the Highlands. But *The Times* reporter believed that they would all soon be reduced to pauperism.[10] In fact we do not know what became of the people of Glencalvie – their role was to illuminate the plight of the Highlanders for one brief moment in 1845. Their eventual fate, as with most of the refugees of the Highland Clearances, is unknown.

There was, however, a sequel to the Glencalvie story. *The Times* reporter continued his tour of the Highlands for another eighteen months, and in October 1846 (as the potato famine was beginning to be perceived in the north) he returned to the Ardgay region. He recollected the publicity that accompanied 'that case of cold-blooded cruelty which excited universal disgust and reprobation'. He recorded that the landlord, Robertson of Kindeace, had let the glen to a sheep farmer named Munro. He also noted that 'weeding out people' was now more cautiously followed but had not been abandoned.

> It is dangerous to turn out twenty families at once; it acquires an awkward publicity, and the shame attaches where it ought. Now, however, the proprietor has hit upon a novel expedient of carrying out 'the principle' of extermination, whilst he hopes to escape both the publicity and the shame. He has contrived a convenant in the lease of the farm to Mr Munro, with a special clause in it, binding him 'to *turn away two families every year, until the complement of cottars is extirpated*'. I have taken the pains to ascertain the accuracy of both these instances of the way the people of the Highlands are 'encouraged' before I have thought fit to make them public.[11]

The landlord, in an attempt to divert unpopularity, transferred the odious work of eviction on to the shoulders of the sheep farmer.

The threat of adverse publicity began to curb the full exercise of landlord power in the Highlands in these years, but there remained many instances of eviction untempered by the fear of public indignation. It was not for another three decades that the public outrage against the excesses of the landlords mounted into a co-ordinated opposition to clearance. By then most of the clearances had already been executed and the campaign became a matter of recovering lost territory. Limiting the power of the landlords was at all times a task larger than the forces the crofters alone could muster.

II. Strathconan

By the mid-nineteenth century much of the Highlands had already been more or less cleared though the population of the region had not yet begun its actual decline. Over the remnants of the Highland peasantry the possibility of clearance hung like the Sword of Damocles. Although some communities raised a degree of resistance to their landlords at the moment of clearance, most acquiesced in their fate. Moreover the very fear of clearance caused some Highlanders to adopt an attitude of extreme deference to their landlords, presumably in the hope that the Sword might be stayed, or employed elsewhere. Some landowners, even some of the parvenu class who had recently bought their way into Highland property, tried to maintain the forms of landlord–tenant relations which they associated with the Highland tradition of clanship. There was an expectation that the people would treat the lairds with the passionate loyalty and sentimental regard evoked in the historical novels of Sir Walter Scott. It produced some extraordinarily anachronistic behaviour and various hollow demonstrations of fealty, even in the late nineteenth century.

The Strathconan clearances in the 1840s demonstrated this theme in the social relations between laird and tenants in the atmosphere of eviction. One of the least edifying consequences of the Strathconan story was the obsequious demeanour of that part of the tenantry that had escaped the clearance. While most of their fellow tenants were cleared off the estate, those who remained clung to their lands, and kow-towed to their landlord on all possible occasions. It was an authentic illustration of landlord authority in the Highlands.

Strathconan, an extensive and beautiful estate in Easter Ross, belonged to the Balfour family which, later in the century, produced a Prime Minister, Arthur James Balfour. They were immensely rich. The wealth of the family – landowners in Fife in the eighteenth century – was gathered together mainly by the efforts of James Balfour (1773–1845). His was a classic case of a second son who carved out a lucrative career in India. In about 1803 he secured a contract with the Admiralty to supply provisions to the British Navy when in Indian waters. In less than ten years he had accumulated an astonishing fortune of £300 000. 'The Nabob', as he came to be called, married into the aristocracy in 1815, and two years later he became a Lowland grandee when he bought the Whittinghame estate in East Lothian. In 1824 he managed to buy part of the family's ancient estate at Balgonie, and in 1839 he added Strathconan in the north-eastern shoulder of the

Highlands. It was a fine collection of estates now commensurate with his fortune: he became the landed gentleman, a builder, Deputy Lieutenant and Member of Parliament. On his death in 1845 he left a fortune well in excess of a million pounds. His son and heir was James Maitland Balfour (1820–56), educated at Eton and at Trinity College, Cambridge, father of the future Prime Minister. He was described by one biographer as

> a handsome, dashing and athletic young man whose charm, however, was liable to sudden dissipation by bad temper.

He became a railway director and also a Member of Parliament, and reorganised the East Lothian yeoman cavalry. He married the second daughter of the second marquis of Salisbury. As a modern writer points out, the Balfours considered their Highland estate overpopulated but in their personal lives they saw no need to practise Malthusian restraint: Lady Blanche bore nine children in eleven years.

Balfour was 'a country gentleman' but otherwise 'a man of no great mark'. He and his father were responsible for wholesale evictions in the Highlands. His son, Arthur Balfour, was Secretary of State for Scotland at the time of the so-called Crofters' War in the mid-1880s. He had considerable personal knowledge of the Highlands, and Gladstone was one of many political guests whom Balfour invited north to enjoy the splendid sporting facilities at Strathconan.[12]

The transformation of the Strathconan district had begun in the first years of the century, before the advent of the Balfours. In 1803 James Hogg reported that extensive farms in the district had been created for sheep farmers and many people were ousted by the change. However, the proprietor reserved a 'small division on the lower end . . . for the accommodation of such of the natives as could not dispose themselves to better advantage'.[13] This was a familiar version of the clearances, a halfway house in terms of eviction and improvement, rarely benefiting the people relocated. It is likely that the descendants of these earlier Strathconan people were among the subjects of the Balfour clearances several decades later.[14]

The removal of people from Strathconan, conducted at various times in the 1840s, is documented in only fragmentary fashion.

The new sequence of evictions was initiated while the property was under the control of trustees and their factor. When the young Balfour came of age he continued the removals. The people to be cleared were not in arrears of rent; their lands were required for the benefit of two incoming sheep farmers – one from Moray, the other a local man. Many of the displaced people were granted asylum on neighbouring estates, or on the arable lands of the Black Isle to the east. Alexander Mackenzie later calculated that, in the course of these clearances, the Balfours removed perhaps 500 people from their lands at Strathconan. Some of them had been subjected to the devastation of a second and even a third clearance as they were shifted across the estate over the course of several years. Mackenzie, without the benefit of evidence, claimed that they had been in comfortable circumstances before being cleared.[15]

The Strathconan clearances, like those of Glencalvie, generated heated controversy in the Highlands. The *Inverness Courier*, in August 1850, sent a reporter to the district to gather an 'impartial' narrative of recent proceedings. Most newspapers were not interested in such wearying detail or in setting the context of a clearance – the drama of the eviction invariably swamped the conditions which had created the event. But the *Courier* provided not only an eyewitness account of the actual episode of clearance but also the essential context of the events.[16]

The facts about Strathconan were well established. There is no doubt that clearances were executed and that houses were demolished by the estate authorities. Seven groups of tenants were shifted at Whitsun 1849 at the termination of their leases. The *Courier* report gave particular attention to the farm of Blarnabee which was accessible only by bridlepath and a ford. In this place had lived five families of tenants on leases; there were also three families of sub-tenants, and four 'parcels' of squatters who paid rent to nobody: altogether there were fifty-eight people in this community. The tenants were collectively responsible for the payment of a rent of £100; the grazing was allocated in shares between them. Until 1849 they had owned stock valued at £700. In his investigation of this case the *Courier* reporter discovered that, in 1844, the tenants had asked the landlord to buy their stock and to take the farm of

Blarnabee off their hands. This resolution may have been caused by disagreements among the tenants. The request was declined; however, the people renewed it in 1847. Balfour had then just appointed a new factor, Smith, from Nairnshire, who advised him to accept the request and pay the people £700 for their animals.

The understanding in 1847 was that the tenants would stay at Blarnabee until 1849, but would hold only the arable land. During the interval they would make arrangements for their future accommodation away from the farm. Two of the tenants negotiated other farms from Balfour. Another four of the families were allowed to stay, either because they were too old to move or were employable locally. That accounted for thirty-one out of an entire population of fifty-eight. The other six families, on being cleared from the estate, settled at Kirkhill, Knockfarrel,[17] Beauly and elsewhere, but mainly in Easter Ross. 'It was a rule from the first, in the proceedings, that no widow or helpless person should be removed from the estate.' These Blarnabee people were among a total of twenty-one families removed from the Strathconan estate on Whitsun 1849. They were mainly sub-tenants and squatters.

The Strathconan estate, like most Highland property, accommodated many squatters in addition to the official tenantry. These were the most awkward class in Highland society, without rights, without history, and usually without friends. The influx of squatters almost certainly reflected the mobility of Highlanders displaced by earlier clearances, as well as the accumulating effects of population growth. Farms which originally had been leased to two tenants were found to possess fifteen families – usually cottars who had little access to land on their own account. By 1850 a population of 116 families (508 people) on the Strathconan estate had been reduced by twenty-seven families to eighty-nine (385 people). Balfour planned further removals for Whitsunday 1850 when the rest of the estate would be brought into rational order.

The *Courier* reporter regarded these clearances as the restoration of a sensible balance between people and land in the glen. The policy had not been prompted by the demands of deer or grouse; it was a consequence, he said, of the indolence of the common people and the sub-division of land by them. Balfour luckily possessed an income which permitted him to improve and rearrange Strathconan without the usual financial constraints which dominated Highland estate management. He was, said the *Courier*, motivated by a wish to establish the long-term security of welfare for the people. This necessitated the reduction of the total population and their reinstatement in a more stable economic order. The actual operation had been planned with the greatest care and the resettlement of the people was generously subsidised. It was a process of reform rather than the pursuit of gain (neglecting at this point to mention the requirements of the incoming sheep farmers). Where possible the people displaced from the glens would be trained into new ways of regular employment and better knowledge of agriculture. Best of all, they would become day labourers.

But despite these precautions the clearances at Whitsunday 1850 attracted adverse attention to the Balfour estate management. Some of the people had been reluctant to leave, even to the point of passive resistance. The estate managers found it necessary 'to call in the services of a Sheriff's Officer and his men to give the proprietor possession of the houses occupied by those people'. The *Courier* said that 'lurid reports' of cruelty had been put about, but were absurd: the law had been used with the greatest hesitation; the people had been given extra time in which to leave; and 'only three houses were pulled down in the whole glen, and only four families, who refused to give a promise to remove at any definite time, were ejected by the officer'. The remainder promised to leave by Lammas. All except a few of these had departed by the appointed time.

The *Courier* reporter decided to witness the final event in this process. This was the clearance of Donald Cameron and a few others. His report spared no detail:

Mr Smith [the factor] and I rode to Blarnabee early in the forenoon, and found the officer and his two assistants and two of the servants from Dalbreck waiting at the foot of the small hill on which the little town stood. The officer first proceeded to the house of Mrs Campbell . . . A daughter came to the door on the officer's summons, and promised, if let alone, to remove the lighter furniture herself. On this promise he proceeded to the hovel – it deserves no better name – of Donald Cameron, who had taken a house at Beauly. He said he had not removed because the house wanted new thatch, and he had no cart to take his furniture. Mr Smith then offered to leave him undisturbed if he could get security that he would remove in eight days, and at the same time offered to convey his furniture to his new house at the end of the time specified. This was agreed to. 'The elder' was then sent for, and, on the promise being repeated to him, the grey haired and very venerable-looking old man gave his hand to Mr Smith as Cameron's security, and the officer passed on. In a byre, formed of branches of trees, so open that every breath of wind blew through and through the house – a place so unhouselike that it was lighted only by the sunshine that entered at the numberless crevices – in this place was found a woman who had been ejected in June, and whose house had then been pulled down . . . She had the choice of her brother's house [at Kirkhill] or of going on the poor's roll, the inspector having provided a place for her at Dingwall, but she would do neither. She was again ejected, and sat silently mending her stocking, whilst the men removed her furniture – following, without a word, when all was out, and sitting down in the sunshine to continue her labour silent as before. The door was locked, and the officer again proceeded to the house of Mrs Campbell. No promise could be got from the woman to remove at any time. I saw the sad glance the poor daughter cast to the green hill before her as she said the words – it revealed the deep sorrow of her heart to leave the scene for ever; but I felt, whilst sympathising with her, that the Allwise Creator had permitted few of his rational creatures to indulge feelings of this nature in profitless idleness. No promise to remove could be obtained, and, assisted by the women, the furniture was removed. Whilst this labour was proceeding, one of the sons appeared from a neighbouring house and lent a hand. When the furniture was removed, he pulled out the window frames, threw down the roof, and pushed in the walls. So little animosity did he seem to feel, that he was most anxious to 'treat' the officers to 'a dram'. This they refused; but all three – mother, son and daughter – joined the officers in the refreshments, drinking 'good health' to all round.

The reporter described this episode at length because he believed it demonstrated that the people who were being ejected did not believe themselves cruelly used, and that it had been conducted 'in a creditably humane spirit'. He considered that the landowner, Balfour, had been subjected to much rabid denunciation which had little foundation in reality.

The *Courier*'s report of the Strathconan clearances was highly sympathetic: its description placed the entire episode in the best light. Moreover the account stressed the positive aspects of the management at Strathconan. For instance, Balfour required all his large tenants to be resident on the estate; he had established a number of club farms with improved cottage accommodation for the people who remained on the property; a schoolroom, with a Free Church teacher, was also provided. Crofts were set at low rents. Trenching and liming schemes were set afoot at a cost of £700. The *Courier* reporter concluded his investigation by saying that removals, 'under any circumstances and however carried out, must bear an aspect of oppression – just as the amputation of a limb seems a cruel thing until its necessity as the only means of cure is considered'. Balfour had acted with great liberality and, though it was a disagreeable duty, he had acted for the long-term benefit of the people. The criticism he had suffered was unfair:

> Supposing the son or daughter of a tenant of a flat in the High Street of Inverness, should marry, and ascending the stairs, settle down in the garret without leave asked or obtained – would any of your readers think it cruel on the part of the landlord to eject the self-made tenant?[18]

The entire Strathconan affair, like so many other such episodes in the Highlands, was disinterred and replayed before the Napier Commissioners in 1883. By then, the population of Strathconan had diminished to about forty tenants. One of the witnesses in 1883 recollected that the threat of removal had been an annual danger, but that he had eventually received a lease. Yet, in the same breath, he said that he was

> consoled by the thought that he lived under the proprietorship of one of a race who proved themselves worthy of being remembered for good; for their names were never connected with anything despicable or mean, such as wholesale eviction on the lots – and I am proud to acknowledge that our present proprietor and his excellent partner in life are both noble examples in the north of whatever is good.

The same witness ascribed the clearances to the influence of agents: 'It is all the doing of the factor that we are all now here'.[19] This was a well-tried method of sanitising the reputations of the landlords from the actions of their minions. The memory of these people was not always in accord with the surviving evidence. Thus, for example, another witness before the Commissioners testified that the main clearances on the Strathconan estate had happened before the Balfours took possession – probably in 1834, he thought, 'when a general clearance in Strathconan under gross circumstances sent the people adrift'.[20] The oral memory was a slippery source though the general shape of events survived in the collective consciousness.

In reality the Strathconan clearances stretched across several decades and the process accelerated when leases expired, as in the later 1840s. There had been a succession of episodes of removal, the circumstances of which varied and are little documented. The tenantry nursed a feeling of grievance against the owner, and even more, against the factors. It was a legacy which remained alive into the 1880s.

After decades of apprehension and fear of removal, the psychological condition of the remaining tenantry was so nervous that they were disproportionately grateful for any token of kindliness from their landlord. In the year of the clearances, in early September 1850, the *Inverness Courier* described the people's reception of the Balfours on their arrival in Strathconan for the late summer season:

They were received at a distance from the lodge by the small tenantry of the glen, to demonstrate the sense they entertain of Mr Balfour's uniform kindness to them. When the carriages came to a halt in the middle of the crowd, the gardener, at the request of the people, addressed the laird and expressed their happiness at seeing him and his lady once more amongst them. Mr Balfour thanked them for their good wishes, and assured them that though it had been considered necessary to remove some of their friends from the glen, it was not more for his interest than for theirs, and expressed the hope that no more removals would ever be necessary, and that they would all be more comfortable now than before. The address was received with a cheer – the horses were taken from the carriage, the people clustered about it, and it was drawn at a rapid pace to the Lodge, the people cheering all the way. At the Lodge Mr Balfour again thanked the people for the compliment they had paid to him and Lady Blanche, which he would not soon forget. Refreshments were then provided, and the health of the laird, of the lady, of the young laird, and other branches of the family drunk with lively demonstrations, and the people separated highly pleased with themselves and the laird.[21]

It was a description that echoed many other accounts of landlord–tenant relations in the Highlands which are, at all times, difficult to reconcile with the general and widely attested tradition of alienation and hatred that was fully exposed in the volumes of the Napier Commission in 1884. Arthur Balfour, later Secretary of State for Scotland and Prime Minister, was said to have been much influenced by his experience in Strathconan. According to his niece he had a personal knowledge of the Highlands:

Strathconan, his own Ross-shire property, had been, when his father succeeded to it, one of the congested areas in the north of Scotland, owing mainly to overcrowding [sic]. In a few years, by temporarily forgoing rents, by expenditure of money on improvements to benefit the remaining tenants, but above all by making arrangements for large-scale emigration the situation of the people was transformed. Balfour spoke of what he knew when he insisted that diminution of population was the only cure for poverty in the crofter districts. The subject interested him, for the welfare of the Strathconan people had absorbed a great deal of his mother's thoughts, and he was very fond of the place.[22]

In his own words, Balfour had 'spent many a night earnestly discussing the hard lot of dwellers in the Highlands and Islands'. He told the House of Commons:

I love and have always loved the Highland population. I have known them from my youth. I have lived among them, and I defy anyone to live among them and not love them. They have to contend with inclement skies, with stormy seas, and with barren soil; and their worst enemies are those who would hinder their superfluous population from seeking in other climes a happier home.[23]

In 1885 Balfour let the Strathconan estate on lease because of his diminished agricultural income, and it was subsequently sold off. His tenants always spoke well of his treatment of them as a landlord, and attributed all their difficulties to injustices of a previous age, episodes about which they had become remarkably vague.

At Glencalvie and Strathconan the clearances were part of a long, punctuated sequence of population displacement. The set-piece evictions attracted sharp public notice but were essentially dramatic moments in a much lengthier process of estate reorganisation which stretched over generations and across changes in ownership. At Glencalvie and Strathconan wealthy owners had delegated authority to local factors whose professional responsibility was to sustain the efficiency of the estate's income. There was in each instance of eviction some destruction of property to prevent the people reoccupying their old houses; there was no violence, no mortality; the people offered little if any resistance and most drifted away in unrecorded exile. These evictions were located in the less impoverished and less congested quarter of the northern Highlands.

There was connection between the two estates: the clearing factor at Glencalvie, Gillanders, bought parts of Strathconan for his own operations. Managerial talent in the Highlands was at a premium in the age of the clearances and men such as Gillanders could swiftly ascend the social ladder and start clearing on their own account.

Glencalvie and Strathconan fall somewhere near the middle of the wide spectrum of the Highland Clearances. At one end were the great mass evictions which required military reinforcement; at the other end were the invisible and silent exoduses which carried much larger numbers away. But in mid-century the population of the Highlands was about to reach its greatest ever numbers: clearance and population increase were, therefore, part of the paradox of displacement. The paradox had much earlier origins which are explored in the next three chapters.

Notes

1   *The Times,* 23 August 1845.

2   *Scotsman,* 19 April 1845.

3   Ibid., 24 May 1845.

4   On the Sutherland clearances see the present volume, chapters 8–11.

5 See Eric Richards, 'How tame were the Highlanders during the Clearances?', *Scottish Studies*, vol. 17 (1973).

6 Mackenzie, *Highland Clearances*, p. 144, quoting Hugh Miller.

7 *The Times*, 20 May 1845.

8 Hansard, *Parliamentary Debates*, vol. LXXI (1845), p. 408 et seq.

9 See for instance, E.P. Thompson, 'English trade unionism and other labour movements before 1790', *Society for the Study of Labour History*, Bulletin No.17 (1968).

10 *The Times*, 2 June 1845.

11 Ibid., 22 October 1846.

12 On Balfour, see *Gentleman's Magazine*, vol. XXIV (August 1845), pp. 200–1; Kenneth Young, *Arthur James Balfour* (London, 1963), p. 15; Sidney H. Zebel, *Balfour, A Political Biography* (London,1973), pp. 1–3; Blanche E. Dugdale, *Arthur James Balfour* (2 vols., London, 1939), vol. I., p. 26; Max Egremont, *Balfour* (London,1980), p. 19; Orr, op. cit., p. 93.

13 Hogg, *Tour*, p. 37.

14 See below, Chapter 8.

15 Mackenzie, *Highland Clearances*, pp. 144–6.

16 *Inverness Courier*, 15 August 1850.

17 See Richards and Clough, *Cromartie*, op. cit., pp. 222–7.

18 Ibid.

19 Napier Commission, Evidence, p. 2660, et seq., evidence of Donald Rain.

20 Ibid., pp. 2668–9, evidence of Finlay Mackay.

21 *Inverness Courier*, 15 September 1850.

22 Dugdale, *Balfour*, pp. 64–5.

23 *The Scot at Home and Abroad*, vol. I, no. 3 (1902), p. 2.

3

The Highland Clearances and Rural Revolution

I. Context

IMAGES OF A PEASANTRY levered out of ancestral homes, of landlords bent on radical change, were neither new nor unique to the Highlands. Glencalvie and Strathconan were symptoms of the great rural changes sweeping across the face of western Europe. The Highlands, like many other parts of the British Isles, were undergoing a long historical transformation. Significant symptoms of the changes in the Highlands can be traced back for at least 100 years, and the region was still divesting itself of people for another hundred. The revolution in agriculture was mostly not by means of dramatic evictions such as those at Glencalvie and Strathconan, but by attrition and stealth, out of sight of the cameras of history.

The pressures for change in the Highlands were eventually greater than elsewhere, the turmoil more fundamental. Change to the entire form of Highland society was forced faster by government fiat after the defeat of the Jacobite uprising at Culloden in 1746. The bloody suppression of opposition in the north created a dramatic context for the reconstruction. It also set the Highland story apart from the normal contexts of rural transformation in the rest of Britain. So too did the relative isolation of the region from many of the earlier modernising forces for agricultural change in the previous century. The distinctive social system of the Highlands, the patterns of local authority, its unusual priorities in the utilisation of its landed resources and the geography itself, all joined to render the Highlands less able to accommodate the urgency for change which descended on all quarters of western Europe in the late eighteenth century. The transformation in the Highlands – most obviously in the clearances – created greater upheaval and ultimately diminished the region's capacity to support its now larger population. Eventually the region found itself with fewer choices for its economic and social future. This was the true origin of the Highland tragedy.

II. *The great change in the nation*

After about 1780 the entire British Isles was enveloped in vast changes and the Scottish Highlanders were unable to insulate themselves from the drama. During this time the country industrialised and increased its population everywhere on a revolutionary scale. The shorthand phrase – the Industrial Revolution – summarises these changes. At the time the cumulative transformation altered all bases of life across the country, even on the outer peripheries and most northerly extremities.[1] The Highlands were not simply the passive victim and receptor of these momentous changes; they were a vital contributor to the change and adjusted as much as, if not more, than the rest of the country to the transition. In retrospect it is clear that the Highlands could never have remained immune from these changes. The region could not, even under a radically different social and political regimen, declare itself outside the shift in the foundations of economic life. The Highlands confronted its own specific problems – poverty and rapid population growth – in a world of larger possibilities than before. But the adjustments were painful and unwanted and very little understood.

Highland geography also set limits to the possibilities of the new age, but the people of the Highlands faced opportunities and alternatives, especially the landlords as the controllers of the region's resources. Landlords had to make decisions about the use of the land and about their own responsibilities for the welfare of the community. The history of the Highlands in the age of the clearances was dominated by the spectre of landlords wrestling with the question of what to do with their estates, as we have seen in the cases of Suishnish, Glencalvie and Strathconan in the latter phases of the Highland revolution.

In the age of the clearances there were landlords who tried to improve agriculture without disturbing or losing their tenantry. Others tried to industrialise their estates, some attempted to subsidise and fructify their Highland properties from the dividends of Empire or opportunistic marriage alliances, both of which were particularly conspicuous in the Highlands. Some lairds closed their eyes to the opportunities as well as to the dangers of economic catastrophe; some of them blustered on until they fell into the widening pit of bankruptcy. Most landlords eventually adopted some variant of the policy of population reduction, having failed to generate new employment and income on their estates. They found their policy choices increasingly choked by circumstances which they could not control. Many of course were like Mr Micawber, simply waiting for something to turn up to save their estates; and as the population rose and crises multiplied, they eventually thought of emigration for their tenantry and even for themselves. This was the context of sheep farming and population displacement, but the story evolved slowly.

The experience of the rural regions in the British Isles was varied – most dramatically different between the south-east of England and central Scotland, and the west of Ireland. The Scottish Highlands had a mixed experience. In 1780 much of the region faced inwards, most of its people living relatively precarious lives with a large dependence on local subsistence production. The region exported black cattle and illicit whisky to southern markets but little else. Living standards were low by any reckoning and the interchange with the rest of the world was still scant. By 1851 much of the Highlands had been converted to sheep production with a fringe of semi-subsistence crofting and some fishing enterprise in a few locations such as Wick and Helmsdale. Meanwhile the Highlands had contributed decisively in the supply of raw wool to British manufacturing, to the great textile mills of Yorkshire. For many decades the Highlands were able to supplement and then replace imports of the raw material of the woollen industry. The region also provided meat to the southern markets as never before, and began importing in a much more varied pattern too. And, throughout, the population revolution had swept over the Highlands; many left the region but the total population of the Highlands continued to rise, if slowly, until 1851. Even where the introduction of sheep had caused most outrage, in Sutherland, the population was greater in 1841 than it had been in 1780. The Highlands were therefore fully committed to the logic of industrialisation, but the roots of the change lay much earlier.

III. Before the clearances

Clearances were not exclusive to the Scottish Highlands; nor were Highland proprietors uniquely prone to evict their tenants and squatters. Clearances were not restricted to the introduction of sheep: landlords shifted tenants in order to extend cattle production, to develop villages, for sporting purposes and for changing forms of arable cultivation. They also cleared estates to reduce population congestion and to lighten the burden of relieving paupers. Nor is it at all certain that the older form of society in the Highlands was in a condition of vitality on the eve of the sheep clearances. Even before the great population expansion of the latter part of the eighteenth century, the capacity of the Highland economy adequately to support its people is questionable.

Contemporary observers were never unanimous about the condition of Highland society before the clearances and modern historians do not speak with a single voice. For instance, Joseph Mitchell knew the Highlands at the start of the nineteenth century better than anyone and he cited approvingly the words of Stewart of Garth, the great defender of old Highland ways. Stewart said that 'a more happy and contented race never existed'. Mitchell himself said that, in pre-clearances days, the people 'led a . . . semi-savage life, disliking industry but enjoying the sports of fishing and shooting which are now esteemed the choice recreation of our aristocracy.' They were 'a kindly affectionate people living a half-idle life'.[2] He also claimed that the Highlanders lived in 'a half wild and uncivilised condition'.[3]

Some of the features of the pre-clearances world of the Highlanders have become better investigated in recent years. The idea that the Highlanders lived in benign opulence and security before the clearances is a seductive myth which bears little relationship to any surviving evidence of the pre-clearance period. Similarly the notion that this was an ageless, static and immobile society is also exploded by all recent historians. Of course those who advocated change in the Highlands always harboured a tendency to exaggerate the failing of the old system, its inequities and its poverty. The opposite applied with equal strength to the guardians of the status quo, the denigrators of change. If there was reciprocity and benevolence of the old order it was balanced by the arbitrary ruthlessness of an extremely hierarchical and bellicose society, one in which low levels of welfare and literacy were accompanied by pre-industrial mortality rates. The reputation of the old order was probably most influenced by the work of Sir Walter Scott who helped to invest the old Highlands with that 'roseate glow' which has hardly yet dispersed. As Leah Leneman says, the romanticisation of the lairds in the early nineteenth century was extraordinary: it was 'a transformation in the popular Scottish consciousness of Highland chiefs from the brutal oppressors of a slavish people they had been pictured as in 1746, to paternal protectors of a grateful peasantry'.[4]

The old Highland order was severely stratified in its social structure, based upon a patriarchal ordering of power which expressed itself in a series of reciprocal obligations and responsibilities. Decisions about the distribution of land and the exaction of services, civil or military, were determined from above. Some historians stress the stability of the old order, with tribal customs subsisting for a thousand years.[5] The idea of the collective clan ownership of the land is unclear, though there can be no doubting the sense of social solidarity that existed in certain districts,[6] and there was a 'system of ideology and behaviour' which pervaded the general mentality. It may have added up to a special variant of the pre-industrial 'moral economy' in which obligations between people and their leaders were more resilient and reciprocal than in modern societies.[7] Whether these ties extended to the submerged sub-tenant strata is more debatable.

At this distance in time the way of life appears autocratically controlled, the people subject to the most arbitrary extractions of services and payments by the masters of the old society – namely the lairds and their henchmen, the tacksmen. It was a pinched framework of life eked out on the narrowest margins of subsistence, though some historians still assume that it gave security to the common people.[8] It was a society in which the main adjudicator of welfare among the people was the fluctuating ratio of population to land. As numbers rose and fell, so the edge of cultivation expanded and contracted. The alternation of good times and bad, of feasting and fasting, fitted the classic model of pre-industrial life, dominated for much of the year by the fear of deprivation in the months before each new harvest.

The exact degree of strain and deprivation is not clear, though it appeared to worsen in the late eighteenth century under the impact of population growth. The new tribes of southern visitors to the north at the end of the eighteenth century were appalled by the squalor they found, though they were equally surprised at the richness of the culture which thrived amid such poverty. Isobel Grant, a writer who explored the inner life of the Highland community with the greatest sensitivity, made no bones about the severity of life in the old Highlands. Referring to the Kingussie–Aviemore district in the 1770s she spoke of the hardness and narrowness of the material conditions typical of 'any starveling, down-trodden peasantry' who lived in conditions 'that would now be considered incompatible with a civilised existence'. The people lived 'on the very verge of absolute starvation', yet it was a life without crime, locks or thieves. It was a simpler and incomparably harsher way of life, relieved, however, by elements in Highland life which were, she insists, 'unspeakably precious'.[9]

Some writers have rebelled against allegedly excessive description of destitution and squalor in the pre-clearance Highlands. Eric Cregeen was especially eloquent in his advocacy of literary and oral sources for a characterisation of that culture. He spoke of

[The] exquisite and highly elaborate music and poetry vigorously alive among ordinary crofters and cottars, and alive not only in the sense of perpetuating an earlier heritage (although it did that) but in the sense of renewing it in creative and socially relevant work.

Cregeen suggested that 'whatever the material conditions of the Highland population of the early nineteenth century, they had nothing of the "slum" mentality and were indeed infinitely more civilised than most of the dwellers of the cities of the plain'.[10] He made an implicit distinction between 'the quality of life' and the material foundations of that life. The combination of extreme privation and a rich culture is, of course, common in peasant societies.

The great variance that exists between observers of Highland conditions derived to a great extent from the inescapable seasonal and annual alternation of good times with hard. As in all pre-industrial societies the weather played a decisive role in economic activity. The annual threat of starvation did not diminish until transport improvements connected regions more effectively. There were times of feast and times of famine and that was the shape of life. A document which described life in Lochaber just after the '45 captured the essence of the society. Speaking of the tacksmen, it observed:

> Each of these has some very poor people under him, perhaps four or six on a farm, to whom he lets out the skirts of his possession. These people are generally the soberest and honestest of the whole. Their food all summer is milk and whey mixed together without any bread; the little butter or cheese they are able to make is reserved for winter provision; they sleep away the greater part of the summer, and when the little barley they sow becomes ripe, the women pull it as they do flax, and dry it on a large wicker machine over the fire, then burn the straw and grind the corn upon quearns or hand mills. In the end of harvest and during the winter, they have some flesh, butter and cheese, with great scarcity of bread. All their business is to take care of the few cattle they have. In spring, which is the only season in which they work, their whole food is bread and gruel, without so much as salt to season it.[11]

IV. Food supply

It was a yearly round of pinching and saving, bounded by the possibility of a lavish harvest or a famine. It was never a secure existence and it is obvious that nature was less liberal to the Highlanders than to the people of the rest of Britain. It was a record of famine – as in 1680, 1688, the 1690s, 1740–1, 1751, 1756, 1782–3 – to mention the most publicised, which exposed the Achilles' heel of the regional economy. By 1700 most of the British Isles was able to produce a reliable supply of food for the majority of the inhabitants, but the shadow of famine still stalked some parts of the land – in 1743–4 Ireland suffered disastrous hunger that killed a high proportion of its people. The harvest of 1772–3 produced a severe shortfall in the north-east Highlands which left an indelible mark on the public mind. It would be remembered with fear for several generations to come, even though the death rate was relatively well contained in the crisis.

The most striking aspect of the society was its underlying anxiety about subsistence – for this was 'a risk laden environment' in which famine was endemic and crops were likely to fail every third year on the average. Dodgshon stresses the extreme insecurity of tenure under the old system. The peripheral small tenantry were 'mere Ephemerae' as Dr Johnson called them.[12] As Dodgshon points out acerbically, 'it was hardly the system suffused with the spirit of a "primitive communism" that some have attached to it'. Migration related to poor harvests in the 1720s and again in the 1770s, though by then there was also a resistance among some of the tacksmen to rising rents and the demands of improvement.[13]

Some historians have ignored the record of famine vulnerability in the Highlands while others claim that it is too easily exaggerated, saying that Highland famine was essentially localised and occasional.[14] In reality the Highlands was the last part of mainland Britain to remain prone to famine, and it retained this awful distinction much later than elsewhere. The growth of the trade in meal, which is not well documented, suggests a strategic and growing dependence on imports. All the evidence about the trade of the Highlands before the clearances is consistent with the picture of an economy closely geared to a dual necessity to export cattle and to import meal. Despite the predominantly subsistence character of economic life, the population had a critical reliance on its trading sector to a degree probably as great as anywhere else in Britain. It was upon these foundations that population growth and structural change were imposed later in the eighteenth century.

V. Paving the way

Old Gaeldom was in transition long before Culloden and the origins of decline and restructuring have been pushed back in time to such a degree that the classic clearances of this book seem to emerge as only the final twists in a much longer story. The sheep simply followed the path long worn into place by internal Highland changes. As one observer has written, it became 'a mobile society moving away from its traditional roots in commercial confidence'.[15]

Even the catastrophe of Culloden has been severely diminished in its historical significance. Allan Macinnes in particular argues that 'Scottish Gaeldom' was already caught in the throes of fundamental change, and this prepared the ground for the later changes associated with the sheep clearances. In the century before Culloden the landlords, the chiefs, were switching from their traditional commitment to clanship and towards a decidedly more commercial use of the lands of the clans. As early as the sixteenth century, the élite of the north were already bending to 'southern values', travelling easily between 'the tribal world of the north and the polite society of the south.'[16] It would eventually subvert the whole structure. Even if it was an external infection it was nevertheless driven by internal choices: 'The picture of a contented society broken by alien forces wholly underestimates the cultural tension within the class prior to the Forty-Five provoked by the commercialising of customary relation by chiefs and leading gentry'.[17]

In essence, the philosophy of heritable trusteeship – which had obliged the chiefs to maintain security of possession within their wide circles of kin – became moribund and rejected. In its place rose the notion of legalised heritable title, which substituted individual for collective possession. It was a deep institutional and psychic change in the very fabric of Gaelic society which, in practical terms, subverted the traditional forms of multiple tenancy under the wing of the tacksmen (the middle stratum of the Highland society) and which connected upwards in an unbroken line of reciprocation to the chief, the patriarch of the people. In Macinnes' words, this was the ultimate source of the 'inexorable reorientation of estates towards the market at the expense of clanship throughout Gaeldom'. It was, in a phrase, the penetration of the old society by the forces of capitalism, which the chiefs gathered enthusiastically to their individual bosoms. It meant that clanship was not a society frozen in time, awaiting the Enlightenment, but a society already shifting: it was not monolithic, static nor underdeveloped.[18]

Robert Dodgshon depicts the change in similar but more ecological terms. He traces an even longer transition in Gaelic society, back into the sixteenth century, a society in continual movement and adjustment to conditions inside and outside the Highlands. He portrays the old Highlands in terms of its distinct ideology of behaviour, most clearly marked by its displays of feasting and feuding, habitual ways of life which served as a primitive means of food management and protection against neighbours. It was a social system in which equity and individual autonomy appear to have been subsumed into the clan and its leaders; and welfare was measured in pre-market terms. It was a rents-in-kind system – an economy of direct consumption. It was based on an exchange or exaction of loyalty in return for collective security and a violent attitude to contiguous clans. The chieftainly model was one in which 'the status and wellbeing of the clan [was established] through conspicuous consumption'.[19] Dodgshon says that the Highland chiefs saw themselves, first and foremost, as trying 'to maximise the social product of land rather than its cash returns pure and simple'.[20] But gross inequality seems to have given rise to recurrent hostility between smallholders at the base of the society.

Security and stability were not easily achieved and research among surviving records of land occupation under the old order suggests a surprising turnover of tenants year by year as well as a remarkable degree of change of actual ownership. It leaves an impression that security of tenure was uncommon and that continuity of occupation was unusual even in normal times. There was 'no great stability from one generation to another' and the cottars and unofficial populations of the estates were the most vulnerable and disposable of all.[21] The tenantry were in a 'continuous state of flux'.[22]

This system was in the grip of long-term transformation, most of all in the mentality of the leadership which, like those of the south, became progressively commercial long before the eighteenth century and therefore before the clearances. The heart of the matter was in 'the growing evaluation of estate resources in purely economic terms' rather than the status conferred in the older system. The ideology of chieftainly behaviour had been decomposing for a very long time.[23] By the end of the eighteenth century, 'the management policies of even the most conservative estate had become dominated by the opportunities of the marketplace and the need to maximise estate income'. By then it had become a society in 'a state of continual movement and adjustment'; since about 1493 it had been responding progressively to the urge to market surpluses.[24]

The crust of customary Gaeldom was, therefore, already broken by the time of Culloden; the chiefs had already been commercialised, the system was overthrown from within by its own leaders. But the changes proceeded at different velocities in different parts of the Highlands.

Rather than a society collapsing under its own weight, there was a growing engagement with commerce and enterprise within and outwith the Highlands, often in surprisingly dynamic form. The socio-economic differences between the Lowland and the Highland gentry were narrowing, and this was greatly hastened by the rapid rise of the cattle trade with England before Culloden. Old tenurial understandings were overturned, demonstrated by the 'piecemeal phasing out of the old tacksmen', or their conversion to the system itself.[25] It was shown eventually in the vigorous entrepreneurship of the traditional leaders, and Highland élites were heavily engaged in profit making across the Empire, in the East and West Indies, channelling capital back to the Highlands. It was demonstrated most tellingly in the commercial exploitation of livestock and the market orientation of the tacksmen.

If the Highland élite was already well travelled along the capitalist road, Culloden remains the greatest convulsion in the breakdown of the old Gaeldom. The British government pursued a policy designed without compunction to modernise and straighten Highland society, to drag it into the wider world of the eighteenth century and to pacify the region. After 1746, it was unashamedly a central policy to destroy those elements in the Highlands that might repeat the military threat to the state. The elimination of the threat was done with brutality: it was a hammer blow to Highland society. The punishment and humiliation meted out also rendered the Highlands less resistant to economic and social change. The Jacobite Rebellion and the subsequent exposure of conditions in the extreme north of Britain turned the Highlands into an arena for the exercise of civilising missions and, especially, economic improvement. In psychological terms the Jacobite crisis helped to confirm the image of the Highlanders as a barbarian menace to the rest of Britain; it reinforced the notion of racial inferiority which all the subsequent romanticism of Samuel Johnson and Sir Walter Scott did not fully dispel.

Macinnes proclaims these events as the last act in the 'ethnic cleansing' of the Highlands, sealing its fate as a system, by means of state terrorism, crass brutality, devastating savagery, psychotic slaughter and systematic repression – all part of a general campaign of 'genocidal slaughter'.[26] Historians in general do not deny or diminish the slaughter of Culloden. As one of them says, 'Following the '45, and given conditions in international politics and diplomacy, it was inconceivable that disloyalty in the Highlands would be left to fester and weaken the British State'.[27] And it was symbolised in the great fortress at Fort George and the other military works in the Highlands. Nevertheless, while the Hanoverians transparently sought to break the back of resistance in the Highlands, there was no serious effort to extirpate and eliminate the indigenous population. In the aftermath the main thrust of policy was expressed less coercively in bringing 'civilisation' to the Highlands, promoting economic, cultural and legal changes from above. The encouragement of the Free British Fishery Society was one 'ideal vehicle for transforming the Highlander from the state of savage barbarism into the embodiment of industry and contentment.' Highlanders would be 'reborn as hard-working and, even more importantly, loyal subjects'. Walter Scott absorbed the later version of this doctrine and in November 1811 endorsed the idea of rapidly converting the Highlanders into 'a new race', a 'quiet and peaceable peasantry' more appropriate to the times.[28]

If there were genocidal instincts at work in the Highlands there were also efforts to re-mould the north and reinforce the unity of the land by positive policies of redevelopment as well as violent subjugation. Moreover after 1750 the native population of the Highlands grew at rates never before experienced in the region, and the government and the élite did everything they could to retain and reinforce the local population. Estates forfeited by Jacobite landlords were the focus of this state-enforced improvement and rationalisation and it entailed the dissolution of much of the old structure, for example the abolition of runrig, the elimination of the tacksmen, the re-location of the population and the termination of feudal exactions. More positively, the process required the introduction of new crops and modes of production, the creation of industrial ventures, the development of roads and other communications, the extension of marketing arrangements, the construction of new villages and the resettlement of the population. The balance between these negative and positive aspects varied widely across the Highlands. There is good evidence that, even before the clearances, little of this transformation was either understood or welcomed by the common people of the region. Many of these changes, on forfeited estates and beyond, began in earnest long before the classic age of the clearances. Some of it was geared to the continuing expansion of commercial cattle production which was driving up rents and causing displacement in many parts of the Highlands.

Culloden and its aftermath stimulated the landlord élite in the Highlands to look outward, to the south, and towards new forms of enterprise. Their involvement in military service eventually became celebrated and new enterprise emerged in many corners. As Macinnes points out, the transatlantic migrations out of the Highlands were themselves often led by ambitious tacksmen and were 'an expression of indigenous enterprise'; the involvement of Highlanders in the Empire was disproportionate, as was the growth of improvement investment in the region. Macinnes sees all this as the ongoing assimilation of the clan élite into the Scottish landed classes and a full commitment to Empire. As he points out, clearance and estate reorganisation was widespread before the coming of the sheep clearances. Symptomatic was the employment of professional surveyors in the 1760s, the harbingers of economic transformations. Land changed hands more swiftly, and tenants bid against each other as rents rose – leaving some tacksmen disgruntled and footloose.

The vitality of Highland enterprise was best expressed in the return of imperial adventurers with their bounty of Empire to plough into their Highlands estates. Sir Alexander MacLeod bought the island of Harris in 1778 and initiated the transformation of the fishing industry, using monies from his career in the East India Company. Similarly, Sir Alexander Campbell of Inverneil, as Governor of Jamaica and Madras, and Neil Malcolm of Poltalloch, as a colonial planter in Jamaica, both reaped large returns which they ploughed back into their Highland properties.[30] The record suggests that an 'indigenous commercial capitalism' had emerged before the 1780s and the clearances, and had already broken the old system. By then many landlords had already 'engineered the first phase of clearances' and had taken the Highlands along the path of capitalist development. Only later did they abdicate this role to incoming elements from the south, mainly after 1815. Indeed many of the early efforts to promote change were aborted and much of the indigenous investment was finally not productive. Many efforts, private and public, suffered very high failure rates. The entire history of the modern Highlands is pockmarked with broken schemes for development, with dreams of economic growth, fishing, manufacturing, mining, villages and new rural enterprise, mainly dashed by the problems inherent in the region's geographical disadvantages.

Indigenous enterprise was stirred to a new intensity but the outcomes mainly disappointed. An early English enterprise to develop Highland resources failed despite substantial investments.[31] Most subsequent problems related to distance from markets and the paucity of marketable resources, but social resistance was substantial, though hardly unique to the Highlands. Rural conservatism was rife and there were ingrained attitudes which constituted a 'crust of custom'. They included oppressive requirements which were exacted by tacksmen. The very idea of sheep farming was regarded as unacceptable by some farmers. In 1767 it was reported that:

> Just now a Farmer thinks it below his Dignity to acknowledge he has any Sheep or knows anything about them; when any Questions are asked concerning them, he Answers: 'I do not know, my wife has Sheep with Leave.'[32]

Nevertheless even the old runrig economy, especially in the southern Highlands, was adjusting towards the commercialisation of production and both cattle and sheep numbers increased in the years 1730–1800. The old system was accommodating to the new stimuli from outside, and especially the growth of sheep production within the old system as the new breeds spread north after 1755. As Dodgshon puts it, the old system was 'market testing a system of farming' that eventually proved to be its own undoing.

VI. *The pastoral problem*

The eventual success of sheep farming in the Highlands created an inescapable paradox. This was essentially a technical problem: the old system of subsistence was highly labour intensive and absorbed the population; the pastoral economy would eventually economise on the second most available resource of the region, namely its labour. In the final analysis the market forces drove the Highlands in the direction of pastoralism, which had little call on the labour supplies of the region, while simultaneously the population built up, partly encouraged by landlords still committed to the mercantilist doctrines of population retention.

In the first phase landlords and producers shifted towards commercial cattle production for southern markets and, though dislocative, this mode of production employed large sections of the local population. By the late seventeenth century the tacksmen of Argyle were being drawn into commercial cattle production and in 1669 there was an early mass eviction of tenants from the islands of Shuna, Luing, Torosay and Seil. Campbell of Knockbuy was involved in cattle production by the 1720s. Money rents spread widely in the century after 1640 and landlords became increasingly attached to the rent-maximising modes of the south. Dodgshon has registered the shifts in the debt structure and ideology of the landlords: tastes, habits and lifestyles changed.[33] It is a picture of a society attempting first to adjust to market opportunities and then later to the strains of population pressure. And there were always great tensions between the needs of the stock economy and the use of the arable land available to the community – 'the inner conflict that existed between the needs of the arable sector and those of the livestock sector'.[34]

Cattle production, as we will see, created turmoil but was mostly able to exist in parallel with the subsistence sector of the economy and even increased employment and income opportunities. Sheep production, from the 1760s onwards, was different and much less assimilable. With sheep the wintering problem required townships to forgo much or all of their low land and literally displace the human inhabitants.

At the start, in the southern Highlands, the expansion of sheep farming was relatively slow, with quite small flock sizes; moreover landlords were hesitant about the social costs of the change. Many of the farms continued to run cattle and horses as the sheep came in. The comparative advantage of sheep over cattle and arable was not finally asserted and there was oscillation between the two.[35] It was the beginning of a long transition until stock exports generated income and paid rents beyond the capacity of any alternative system. Eventually the sheep diminished the arable capabilities of the people at a time of radical population increase. Inevitably it bred insecurity, competition and dislocation.

Across the rest of Scotland agrarian change eventually had the same effect, that is to reduce the labour requirements in agriculture.[36] The process was more sudden and dramatic in the Highlands and greatly exacerbated by the population increase under way by 1760. As Dodgshon insists, the sheep clearances were essentially an acceleration of the process long in motion, more dramatic and greater in scale but in essence the same process but now the strains were multiplied and the tragedy entrenched.[37] These great conflicts and contradictions were generated between the subsistence requirements of the community and the new demands of the pastoral economy. A great rift emerged between the needs of the landlord (and those tacksmen who had served their commercial apprenticeships before the sheep arrived in the late eighteenth century) and those of the people. The interests of the landlords diverged from those of the lesser tenants progressively. The latter needed to maintain their access to both arable land and cattle pasture, but this came into diametrical opposition with the new pastoralists. There was a conflict between the subsistence requirement of the community and the rent-raising motives of the landlords. Eventually the local producers were too numerous and ill-equipped to deal with the competition from the incoming sheep farmers and they lost their grip on the land.[38]

The fundamental question was whether the Highlands, with either the new or the old system, could ever adequately support its population, even before the great demographic expansion of the late eighteenth century. Opinion is divided but Dodgshon believes that not only was the old feudal system in the Highlands moribund before Culloden but even in the period 1650–1780 population was outstripping the resources of the region. As he says, 'Put in simple terms, the Highlands and Islands had too many people dependent on too little arable land'.[39] The key question was 'whether traditional agriculture on the eve of change was sustainable'. Some observers, like Knox in 1784, saw only 'Seats of oppression, poverty, famine, anguish, and wild despair', and they believed that the old system was manifestly dysfunctional.[40] The modern view is that 'even the most generous could not accept that the social and economic structure should remain intact and unchanged when it was so patently unable to provide the bare necessaries of life in many places for a rising population'.[41]

The new sheep system would not be compatible with the old agriculture. Some landlords tried to deflect the change. In 1800 the adviser to the earl of Seaforth calculated that the entire population of Lewis could be reduced to 120 shepherds and their families and those who could make a living from kelp [that is, seaweed for southern industry] and fishing; but the majority of the remaining 10 000 inhabitants would have no place. Macdonald, in 1802, recoiled from the logic of the market and said that he did 'not want to dismiss great numbers of his tenants'.[42] But the pressures on Lewis and Skye continued to mount and their capacity to cope diminished as the decades passed and the population continued to rise.

VII. The population imperative

The growth of the population of the Scottish Highlands stands at the centre of the story of the clearances, but it is rarely accorded this status. It was the most important single fact of life in the fate of the region throughout the turmoil; it was something which landlords could exacerbate or mitigate but they could hardly control. Whether or not the landowners intervened, the explosive growth of population in the poorest parts of the Highlands placed an unyielding clamp which restricted the possibilities of progress. In essence, the Highlands experienced the general British (indeed West European) expansion of human numbers without any expansion of the economic capacity which accompanied change in the rest of the country, apart from the chilling example of southern Ireland.

The explosive population growth of the late eighteenth century came after a chequered demographic experience in the previous century. The population of the Highlands probably fell by more than a quarter in the famished years of 1696–9, but there was a relative stability of numbers until about 1750. Then the population pressures accumulated much more seriously in the west and north than in the east and south. Indeed, taken together, the population of the Highlands in the century 1750–1850, increased less than that of Scotland as a whole. But in the west and north of the Highlands numbers increased by 34 per cent from 1755–1800, and then by a further 53 per cent before 1841. This was the stark measure of the strain now imposed on a region which, even in the best of times, was notoriously vulnerable to harvest failure and extreme poverty. The critical point is that the increases took place in a purely agrarian setting, one in which for much of the period, Highland industries were dying. The region fell into a Malthusian trap, increasingly unable to support its numbers.

There was a telling contrast. In the south and east of the Highlands, generally the better off and more technically advanced districts, the population grew little at all before 1800 and then only by about 7 per cent before 1840. This blessed stability masked the essential difference which was related to the different rates of migration. From the south and east the Highlanders were easily drawn by the magnetic attraction of the towns and villages of central Scotland, some specifically recruited into the new cotton mills. Highlanders migrated not because of sheep clearances as such but because of accessible employment nearby. As early as 1741 10 per cent of the population of Greenock was Highland-born; by 1791 it was nearly one-third.

From the north and west the movement outwards was much less, despite the long tradition of Atlantic emigration which indeed continued throughout the period.[43] The outflow was never enough to effectively restrain the upward thrust of population along the western littoral. So the population expanded generation after generation, each pressing more heavily on the economic base which itself was shrinking. Eviction and resettlement policies probably exacerbated the problem but were not the first cause. The population of the Highlands was never greater than in the age of the clearances.

In some locations in the west the increases were spectacular. Thus the population of Skye increased from 13 000 in 1772 to 23 000 in 1841; Harris, Lochs, North and South Uist, Applecross and Lochbroom all doubled in population between 1755 and 1841, while in Tiree, astonishingly, the population was 1500 in 1747, 1776 in 1802 and 4453 in 1831.[44] In the Western Isles as a whole the population grew by 80 per cent between 1755 and 1821, often accommodated in a proliferation of small holdings, swelling the number of crofters in the new regime. In one Lewis parish the population increased by almost 28 per cent in the 1830s alone, and then continued to increase by 38 per cent before 1881. Some of the local rates were greater than the average for Ireland in the 1830s.[45]

The meaning was unequivocal. Even without the introduction of sheep farming the region in the north and west confronted an unprecedented crisis of numbers simply because, apart from the production of potatoes, there was no concomitant and consistent growth of food supplies or employment. There were some false hopes which seemed to sustain the population for a few decades – notably the introduction of kelp manufacture and new fishing villages in the west – but there was no reliable growth in the economy. The regiments and the Empire absorbed some of the human surpluses – military service alone accounted for more than 48 000 men between 1756 and 1815.[46] But the resident population continued to grow while employment and subsistence crumbled, leaving the region almost as susceptible to famine as many parts of contemporary Ireland. The fear of famine hung ominously upon the west Highlands and Islands, catastrophe being predicted from 1810, and becoming a reality in 1837–8 and yet more decisively in 1847–51.

The population increases inevitably created congestion, squalor, fear and poverty, even where no clearances occurred. If a landlord wanted to improve his land, or raise his rental income (a standard intention of virtually every landlord across the nation) or improve the condition of his tenantry, his first task was inevitably to reduce the pressure of population on the land. It was an unyielding reality from which there was no escape. It was a matter at the very centre of the Highland tragedy and no landlord and no other agency was able to create conditions in the Highlands which were able to accommodate a dense population at tolerable living conditions. The western Highlands, despite the colourful and well-publicised emigration of hundreds of clansmen, could not cope with the population increases.

The timing of the population increases strongly suggests that the demographic pressure predated the clearances but coincided with the rapid inflation of rents imposed by landlords from 1780 onwards. The signs of land hunger were clear before the sheep encroached and made it worse. As Cregeen remarks, 'Unless new resources were found progressive poverty was inevitable'.[47] Seasonal and permanent migration were expressions of land hunger; recruitment into the regiments was much assisted by the internal pressure of numbers; sub-division and increasing reliance on the potato were further responses. The potato was one of the most important means by which the population growth was sustained without much further diversification of the economic structure. It was a perilous course and much criticised by contemporary ideologues of improvement. On sub-division William Marshall reported that:

The farms were frittered down to the atoms in which they are now farmed: and the country is burdened with a load of tenantry which had hitherto been considered a bar . . . to the prosecution of any rational plan of management.[48]

Thirty years earlier, long before most of the sheep clearances, James Anderson had testified to the burden of population in a description which corresponds with the technical definition of overpopulation. He said categorically that 'there is no doubt that one-tenth part of the present inhabitants would be sufficient to perform all the operations there, were their industry properly exerted'.[49] Some landlords had blundered and encouraged sub-division and early marriage, and – before 1815 – tried to prevent emigration.

There is every indication that the population in the west was pressing towards its Malthusian limit. The island of Coll was a classic case in point. According to a contemporary observer, Coll carried at least one-third too many people. Its proprietor was caught in a dilemma. He could not bring himself to evict the surplus people, yet there seemed no humane alternative except further sub-division and congestion, which would only depress further the average levels of welfare. The sine qua non of any agricultural improvement was the introduction of large tenants with capital. Meanwhile the condition of the people worsened and the landlord was forced to forgo large amounts of rent because he was under 'the necessity of maintaining three or four hundred souls of a superfluous population'. The alternative – viz. 'forcibly driving them away from the dwellings of their fathers, without capital, trade, or any other visible means of subsistence' – was utterly unthinkable. In these circumstances (which were general in the west) Macdonald, the agricultural reporter, believed that the only answer was 'the paternal interposition of the legislature', that is, state intervention to create employment for the redundant population of the Highlands. 'This', he remarked, 'might surely be done without any clamour or noise, without the appearance of violence, or the odium of expatriation.'[50] Macdonald's eloquent pleas are particularly significant because they were written before the decline of the Highland economy; within three years of the publication of his book the entire context of Highland development was much worsened by the effects of depression and long-term decline.

Landlords were increasingly faced with hordes of small tenants who, rather than sources of rental income, were intensifying the burden on the rental finances. They were an unambiguous impediment to a decent return on the capital value of the land. This was a moral and economic dilemma to which great piquancy was added by the vicarious guilt inherited from the actions of fathers and grandfathers who had encouraged the people to multiply to fill the regiments and process the kelp (even where they needed very little encouragement). The exquisite moral problem was sharpened further by the remnants of the old paternal notions of clan loyalty and reciprocation of obligations between landlord and tenant, often enough expressed by lachrymose landlords in the midst of these recurrent crises, and re-romanticised by Sir Walter Scott and Stewart of Garth. When famine descended, in 1847, emigration at last surged swiftly, producing a spectacular response to the needs of the moment.